PLAYING FOR KEEPS

WHAT YOU DO THIS
WEEK MATTERS.

REGGIE JOINER   KRISTEN IVY

orange

"When it comes to parenting or leading children, it's easy to forget what matters most. *Playing for Keeps* is the reminder we all need!"

ANDY STANLEY

Senior pastor, North Point Community Church and author, *Deep and Wide*

"Reggie Joiner has been my friend through a variety of times, and I have watched as he has prioritized for what matters most. *Playing for Keeps* reminds us all that we only have a certain amount of time to spend, and how we spend that time will make all the difference."

JOEL MANBY

CEO, Herschend Family Entertainment and author, *Love Works*

"I want to give this book to every volunteer serving in children's ministry today! What a great way to convince them that what they do year after year in the lives of kids is a significant faith investment. Thanks, Reggie!"

SUE MILLER

Children's ministry expert and author,
Making Your Children's Ministry the Best Hour of Every Kid's Week

"*Playing for Keeps* flips the telescope and helps us look through the other end. When you read the ideas in this book, you won't want to just hug your kids, you'll want to love them linebacker style and tackle them."

BOB GOFF

President and Founder, Restore International and author, *Love Does*

DEDICATION

We could dedicate this book to the kids in our own lives—those who have captured our hearts and inspired most of the words in this book. But you don't know them. So, instead, write down your own list. Who are the kids in your family or circle of influence that compel you to Play for Keeps?

TO:

....

....

....

....

....

I WANT TO GIVE YOU ...

time over time, so we can have a history worth repeating.
love over time, so you will understand your eternal worth.
words over time, so you can have a better direction.
stories over time, so you can imagine a world beyond yourself.
tribes over time, so you will always have a place to belong.
fun over time, so you will have joy that lasts a lifetime.

TABLE OF CONTENTS

YOU CAN'T MAKE A KID
LOVE GOD, HAVE FAITH,
OR CARE ABOUT WHAT MATTERS . . .

. . . BUT YOU CAN GIVE THEM 6 THINGS OVER TIME.

TIME

LOVE

WORDS

STORIES

TRIBES

FUN

YOU CAN MAKE THE KIND OF HISTORY THAT SHOWS
THEM WHY THEY MATTER TO GOD.

6

THINGS

⬇

EVERY KID
NEEDS

OVER TIME

6

HABITS

and

18 SOMEWHAT PRACTICAL IDEAS

So you can make whatever matters matter even more!

IT'S TIME
TO GET
SERIOUS

THIS IS NOT A BOOK ABOUT . . .
managing your time more effectively.
or getting more done in your day.
or adding more to your "be a better leader or parent" list.

INSTEAD, it's a book about why you should keep
doing the things you are already doing for kids.

We assume if you're reading this book,
you already care deeply about children and teenagers.

More specifically, you are interested in this book because you are
serious about helping kids build a better future. You are intentional
about investing in the Simons and Erics of your world.
*(If you don't recognize those names, it means you skipped the fiction
side of this book. So flip it and start over.)*

You may not even be aware why the ordinary things you do every week will matter one day. So, we want to clarify what matters and why it matters.

If you're reading this because someone gave it to you, you've probably realized by now you're being manipulated into caring about children. We think that's okay.

SERIOUSLY.
If you had . . .
a mother who gave birth to you,
parents or guardians who didn't let you starve to death,
or any adult who kept you from running into the middle of a busy street,
then you should be willing to give a little of your time to a kid.

THINK ABOUT
IT THIS WAY:

If you presently exist, it's only because some adult somewhere cared enough to be present in your life. And if someone gave you enough time and attention to help you get where you are, then you should probably do the same for some

sweaty
sticky
smelly
snotty
snobby
selfish
stubborn
CHILD who acts like you did when you were that age.

IT'S SIMPLE REALLY.

We should feel obligated, because we were all kids once.
And if we are still part of the human race, then we are expected to take care of our young.

TO	TO	TO	TO	TO
GIVE	PROTECT	RESCUE	NURTURE	INSPIRE
THEM A	THEM	THEM	THEM	THEIR
SHOULDER.	WHILE	WHEN	WHILE	FAITH.
	THEY ARE	THEY	THEY ARE	
	HELPLESS.	ARE IN	GROWING.	
		TROUBLE.		

AND NOT JUST THOSE OF US WHO ARE PARENTS,
but all of us who are old enough to make a difference.
We are called to be present in the lives of the next generation.

WE ARE ALL RESPONSIBLE.
That's why, this week, some of you will . . .

RIDE A BIKE	THROW A BALL	CHANGE A DIAPER
COOK A MEAL	WRITE A NOTE	TELL A STORY
HOST A PARTY	TAKE A WALK	SEE A MOVIE
CATCH A FISH	TUCK SOMEONE IN	GO TO CHURCH
LAUGH OUT LOUD	SING A SONG	DANCE A DANCE
PLAY A GAME	SAY A PRAYER	OR TAKE A TRIP

If you are honest, sometimes you wonder if any of this really matters.

You think it's . . .
just expected.
part of your role.
what you do every week.

In your real, bland, mundane world,
these tasks seem rather
unremarkable,
ordinary,
and routine.

But what we hope you discover in this book is that there is a secret hidden in the rhythm of your regimen. The gift of your time is much more remarkable than it seems.

That's why what you do this week, and every week, matters.

BECAUSE OVER TIME ...

YOU ARE MAKING A PERMANENT IMPRINT
ON THE SOUL OF A CHILD.
YOU ARE LEAVING A LEGACY.
YOU ARE PLAYING FOR KEEPS.

**IT'S TIME TO GET SERIOUS ABOUT
WHAT YOU DO WITH YOUR TIME.**

IT TAKES

TIME

—— *over* ——

TIME

TO MAKE A HISTORY
WORTH REPEATING

TIME

Matters

TIME

Matters

Several years ago, we handed out jars of marbles to parents
and to leaders who work with kids and teenagers.

THERE WERE 936 MARBLES IN EACH JAR.

936 IS THE ESTIMATED NUMBER OF WEEKS BETWEEN BIRTH AND
HIGH SCHOOL GRADUATION.

Parents and leaders were challenged to reduce the number of marbles in
the jar to match the actual number of weeks they had left with each child.

Then they were given a simple assignment:

REMOVE ONE MARBLE EACH WEEK.

Over time, the practice of losing marbles had a strange effect.

IT REMINDED THEM TO VALUE THEIR TIME.

IT MADE EACH WEEK MATTER A LITTLE MORE.

IT REINFORCED A SIMPLE PRINCIPLE:

WHEN YOU SEE HOW MUCH TIME YOU HAVE LEFT,

YOU TEND TO DO MORE WITH THE TIME YOU HAVE NOW.

If you're a parent you may be thinking,
That's a really stupid idea.
I already feel enough pressure.
I can't wait to be reminded every day that I am running out of time with my kids.

Okay.

Maybe there is a downside to creating a marble countdown clock.
Like . . .
Depression
Guilt
Anxiety
Drinking

SO, YOU COULD CONSIDER THE ALTERNATIVE:

Ignore that time is slipping away, watch a lot of TV, and pretend your kids will never . . .

care about how you dress.
stop eating kids' meals.
be interested in dating.
ask for the keys to your car.

What if you could really find balance between living in total denial that your kids will pack their bags and move out one day and the sheer panic that makes you double-bolt and padlock the doors?

Now, if you're a leader, you may actually be excited about the fact that someone is moving on. (No, of course you aren't.)

A HEALTHY UPSIDE TO VISUALIZING
YOUR TIME IS THAT IT HELPS YOU
STAY FOCUSED ON THE VALUE OF YOUR
RELATIONSHIPS. IT'S POSSIBLE THAT
CREATING A SIMPLE COUNTDOWN
CLOCK WILL BE JUST WHAT YOU NEED
TO REMIND YOURSELF WHAT YOU DO
TOGETHER OVER TIME MATTERS.

DOES THAT MEAN

you have to make every **SECOND** count,
turn every **MINUTE** into a teaching opportunity,
and keep a daily journal to record it all?

——————— Nope. ———————

Not unless you want to drive yourself and those around you crazy.

WHAT ABOUT A MORE PRACTICAL IDEA?
An idea that works for both parents and leaders.

What if you just decide to make history?
One **WEEK** at a time.

What if you start acting like what you do **WEEKLY**
is more critical than what you can do in a **DAY**?

The point is ...

If you are investing in a
kid or teenager,
you are already making history
every week.

The problem is ...

When you're making history,
you usually don't know it.

That's the real reason we are writing this book:
Simply to remind you that what you're doing now matters more than it feels like it does. And that's why this week and every week is really important.

Let's think about it another way.
Most kids don't know what you're doing this week is going to be a formative part of their history.

They are just kids.
They only see "now."

To them you just . . .
built a sandcastle.
took them to swim lessons.
played basketball in the driveway.
saw a movie.
ate some pizza.
cleaned up their . . .
(not sure that's appropriate to write.)

BUT YOU ARE AN ADULT.

You see yesterday, today, and tomorrow.
So, you should know better.
You should realize by being present in their life week after week in a variety of different ways,

YOU ARE ACTUALLY MAKING HISTORY.

It's kind of like a good country song.
Trace Adkins talks about it when he describes a dad taking his
daughter fishing.

"And she thinks we're just fishin' on the riverside
Throwin' back what we couldn't fry
Drownin' worms and killin' time
Nothin' too ambitious
She ain't even thinkin' 'bout
What's really goin' on right now
But I guarantee this memory's a big 'un
And she thinks we're just fishin'" [1]

The good news is you don't have to be a
gifted communicator,
famous musician,
innovative designer,
or savvy entrepreneur
to make meaningful history.

Any parent or leader can do it as long as they decide to show up and
be present week after week in the life of a kid or teenager.

When what you do this week is repeated next week, it will begin to
earn credit in someone's life.

Rome wasn't built in a day.

Okay, I know that's a cliché, but it's true.
Rome was built over 365,000 days.
THAT'S WHAT HISTORY DOES.

History accomplishes something over time that is
UNIQUE
POWERFUL
LASTING
RICH
MEANINGFUL

Some things just can't be accomplished in a day. Or a week.
They take multiple weeks. It takes time over time to . . .
discover a vaccine.
write a novel.
play the violin.
grow a Duck Dynasty beard.
raise a child.

But you have to resist the temptation to take shortcuts. There is no such thing as instant faith or character.

Again, the secret is *time over time*.

Our attraction to immediate results can keep us so busy we never engage in work that has lasting impact. We get so pre-occupied with what we *can* measure, we don't give attention to what we *can't* measure.

Did you ever stop to think:
The reason you can't see spiritual growth is because it's too "spiritual"?
The reason you can't predict pivotal moments is because they are
too unpredictable?

THAT'S WHY
SHOWING UP THIS
WEEK MATTERS.

The best thing you can do is choose to keep . . .
investing in what you can't see.
being present for what is not happening.

trusting that time over time will do what God has designed it to do.

WHAT IF TIME WAS INVENTED AS A
CLEVER WAY TO ACCOMPLISH CERTAIN
THINGS IN LIFE THAT CAN ONLY
HAPPEN OVER TIME?

MAYBE THAT'S WHY IT'S IMPORTANT
TO SEE TIME IN RELATIONSHIP TO THE
PAST, PRESENT, AND FUTURE.

ACTUALLY, A HEALTHY PERSPECTIVE OF
LIFE TAKES THESE THREE TENSES OF
TIME INTO CONSIDERATION.

If time was created, then time obviously matters.
It has a unique purpose in the greater scheme of the universe.

> In other words, it's no accident the earth spins on its equator at
> approximately 1,000 miles per hour, causing the appearance of the
> sun to rise and set with mathematical accuracy.
>
> It's no accident the earth moves through space at a speed
> of 67,000 miles per hour, causing the seasons to change in a
> calculated manner.

The entire universe has a predicable rhythm.

What if understanding those rhythms could help you become more effective at making meaningful history with the people around you?

The cosmos works together like gears on a clock. If we study it, we can evaluate and predict how things
GROW
CHANGE
AGE

It seems obvious that time exists for a purpose.

Have you ever stopped to think that maybe God established time as a platform so He could communicate something so complex that it needed to be presented strategically over time?

Why didn't God send Jesus as soon as Adam and Eve ate the fruit? He could have resolved the issue then and there. But He waited.
He used time.

He gave Abraham a son.
He let Joseph sit in jail.
He sent Moses to deliver a nation.
He let a nation wander in the desert for decades.

Have you ever thought about why?

IT WAS AS IF GOD DECIDED,

I CAN HELP YOU UNDERSTAND
SOMETHING WITH TIME THAT YOU
COULD NEVER REALLY UNDERSTAND IN
A MOMENT.

THERE ARE ASPECTS OF GOD'S NATURE, SECRETS
ABOUT LIFE, AND CODES TO THE UNIVERSE THAT ARE
SO INTRICATE THEY SIMPLY TAKE TIME TO DECIPHER.

If a heavenly Father uses time to clarify and solidify certain values in our hearts over time, then maybe that's the best way to cultivate what matters in the hearts of our own children and the children we serve as well.

The most significant gifts we can give the next generation are what we give them over time. That makes what you do this week, and next week, and the week after, strategic. As parents or leaders, it's important that we realize there are certain things that can only be

Communicated
Understood
Discovered over time.

THAT MEANS
WHAT YOU DO EVERY
WEEK MATTERS
IF YOU KEEP
DOING IT.

REMEMBER . . .

We don't experience worth because we are loved once,
but because we are loved by someone over time.
We are not motivated to action by one phrase,
but by words that move us over time.
We don't understand the world through a single event,
but through a collection of stories over time.
We don't know we belong because of an invitation to something,
but because we have been welcomed in a tribe over time.
We don't discover how to live in a moment,
But we live when we experience the joys of life over time.

THAT'S THE WAY LIFE WORKS.

That's why we hope you never see a week the same
way again. The futures of the kids you love depend on
what you give them over time.

6 THINGS EVERY KID NEEDS

There are certain things kids only get in a weekly relationship with a parent or adult leader. We don't claim to be experts on what every kid needs this week, but we do know at least a few things every kid needs over time. When you combine these things over time, it helps you make the right kind of history.

TIME

over time makes history
worth repeating.

LOVE

over time helps them establish
a healthy sense of worth.

WORDS

over time influence them to keep
moving in a better direction.

STORIES

over time connect them to a bigger
world and shape their perspectives.

TRIBES

over time establish a circle
of relationships where they can
experience belonging.

FUN

over time fuels quality friendships
and personal resilience.

When you harness the collective power of your weeks, it has the potential to change how you see every week.

PLAY *for* KEEPS

HABIT 1

VISUALIZE TIME

*Create physical cues
as reminders*

Evidently there is an advantage to putting a visual number to the time you have left. Sure it may seem a little morbid at first, but according to some, it can be smart. One shrewd leader prayed this prayer:

"TEACH US TO NUMBER OUR DAYS, THAT WE MAY GAIN
A HEART OF WISDOM" (PSALM 90:12).

So, how does counting your days give you a heart of wisdom?
I'm not sure.

But I can guess.
Visualizing time may help you . . .

pace yourself,
narrow your focus,
guard your margin,
value quality interaction,
and become more intentional about what you do.

All of which probably gains points in the wisdom category. It just makes sense that **if you count the days or weeks you have left with kids, you stand a better chance of making them count.**

Do you realize you don't usually watch a clock to see what time *it is*? Instead, you look at it to see how much time *you have left*. As a small group leader of high school girls, I (Kristen) typically make a commitment to stay with the same group for multiple years. Something happened a few years ago when one of my groups was halfway through

their junior year. One Sunday night as I watched these girls worship, I was struck with this thought: *We only have a year and a half left before graduation.* I had already invested more time with them than the time we had remaining. I was past the halfway point, and it made me panic. There was so much I still wanted to do with them and for them. I literally stepped back from worship, found a piece of paper, and just started making a list:

Go on a mission trip.
Be a part of weekly service.
Offer a mid-week Bible study.
Have a party.
Connect with their parents.
Re-connect with . . . (some of the girls I hadn't seen in awhile).

I remember praying over that list. I didn't know if I could make it all happen. I wasn't even sure why it felt so urgent. But I know that day was important for our group. Many of those things made the difference in how we spent our last year and a half together. We did have a party, and it became a tradition for years after they graduated. We did make it a point to serve together, and many of those girls are still serving in churches today. I honestly believe the simple act of visualizing the time we had left made our last year and a half more meaningful.

The point is each week will matter more when you see it in the context of how many weeks you have left with your kids before they move to whatever is next.

Visualizing time can help you emotionally, mentally, and practically prioritize what really matters. That's why keeping a jar of marbles or something else in sight can make a difference.

THINK ABOUT IT. WHEN YOU ADD
A COUNTDOWN CLOCK TO ANY GAME,
COMPETITION, OR EXERCISE, IT
AFFECTS BEHAVIOR. NEXT TIME YOU
WATCH A BASKETBALL TEAM,
SEE IF YOU NOTICE WHAT HAPPENS
TO THEIR . . .

ENERGY • FOCUS • PASSION

AS THE CLOCK GETS CLOSER TO ZERO.

A FEW IDEAS ...

COUNT IT DOWN

Go ahead and try it. Count down the number of weeks you have with a kid or teenager before they transition to what's next.

Create a countdown clock and put it where you can see it on a consistent basis. You can fill a large jar or container with objects (marbles, paper clips, M&M's™, Jelly Bellys®, gum balls, etc. *Warning: Edible items may disappear faster than a week at a time.*)

Or you can create a digital countdown clock on a smartphone or desktop. One free app designed specifically for this purpose is *Legacy Countdown.* Parents can count down how many weeks they have until a son or daughter graduates. Leaders can count down how many weeks they have until a kid transitions to another ministry.

Here are some general numbers to get you started. When a child is born, you have approximately 936 weeks before he or she graduates from high school. Then every year that follows will look similar to this chart.

1 yr ....884 weeks	7 yrs............572 weeks	13 yrs..........260 weeks
2 yrs...........832 weeks	8 yrs...........520 weeks	14 yrs.........208 weeks
3 yrs...........780 weeks	9 yrs...........468 weeks	15 yrs.........156 weeks
4 yrs...........728 weeks	10 yrs.........416 weeks	16 yrs.........104 weeks
5 yrs...........676 weeks	11 yrs.........364 weeks	17 yrs.......... 52 weeks
6 yrs...........624 weeks	12 yrs.........312 weeks	18 yrs........... 0 weeks

Some families simply create a marble countdown to serve as a reminder. Some parents even design a weekly ritual (like a meal or prayer) around removing a marble each week.

A number of leaders keep a container of marbles on their desk to represent how many weeks they will have a kid or teenager in their ministry.

No matter how we visualize time, it has a psychological effect on how we prioritize time.

MEASURE IT OUT

Sometimes it helps to visualize time as if it were a music score. A week is similar to a measure within a song. Every week has the same amount of time, yet every week can have a different emphasis. As parents and leaders, you have the potential to establish a rhythm within each week that sets up a pattern for your kids. Remember, just like it takes multiple measures to create a song, it takes multiple weeks to establish history together. So, if you want a better history, change what happens this week.

PARENTS, START WATCHING THE FLOW OF YOUR WEEK AND IDENTIFY THE BEST TIMES TO . . .

create breaks,
plan activities,
go to church,
eat meals,
do chores.

LEADERS, START THINKING ABOUT THE BEST WEEKLY OPPORTUNITIES TO INVEST IN KIDS.
Learn how to cooperate with the rhythms that exist in the average kid's or teenager's schedule this week so you can connect in relevant and practical ways. Think about the hours you spend with kids and teenagers in the context of their week.

BASICALLY,
LEARN TO READ AND
IMPROVE THE RHYTHM
OF THE WEEK.

ONE WAY TO CELEBRATE STRATEGIC WEEKS IS TO RECOGNIZE THE MILESTONES THAT HAPPEN IN THE LIVES OF KIDS. WE DECIDED TO SYMBOLIZE THEM WITH SIX UNIQUE MARBLES IN OUR JARS. YOU CAN ADD OTHER MILESTONES YOU FEEL ARE SIGNIFICANT; JUST RECOGNIZE THESE REPRESENT A FEW OF THE IMPORTANT EVENTS THAT HELP DEFINE A CHILD'S IDENTITY BEFORE THEY LEAVE YOUR HOME OR MINISTRY.

A DEDICATION MARBLE
symbolizes a dedication service
or first birthday

A TRANSITION MARBLE
symbolizes coming of age
(*Do I have to explain?*)

A WISDOM MARBLE
symbolizes the first day of
school or the beginning of
primary education

A FREEDOM MARBLE
symbolizes getting a driver's
license and stepping toward
independence

A FAITH MARBLE
symbolizes a decision to trust
Christ, Baptism, or Confirmation

A GRADUATION MARBLE
symbolizes completion of
secondary education

We use a unique Milestone Marble so it stands out in the collection of weeks along with a special marble that symbolizes birthday weeks. To celebrate milestones and birthdays, marbles are removed and put in a special container or bag to indicate they have happened.

MARK IT UP

What if you mark up a calendar to highlight significant events and weeks? Build a routine in every week to preview what's coming on the calendar and update it weekly. You may discover taking the time weekly to mark up your calendar can actually help you anticipate and celebrate important weeks. Two marbles in a jar can look similar, but no two weeks are created equal. Some weeks are . . .

birthday **weeks.**

starting school **weeks.**

end of school **weeks.**

holiday **weeks.**

vacation **weeks.**

special event **weeks.**

With a little initiative, you can highlight and anticipate some important weeks. Just giving those weeks a little extra attention can create a great collection of memories for your family or your group.

Oh, two more things.

WEEKENDS WEREN'T MADE FOR MICHELOB

Weekends were made for relationships. The number of weeks you have left in your jar, bucket or calendar before your kids transition also represents the number of weekends you have left. So, guard them. The next time someone asks, "Do you have plans for the weekend?"—have an answer. Weekends are very strategic in building a positive history together.

SUNDAYS AREN'T JUST FOR FOOTBALL

Okay. Sundays can be for football, too. But Sundays are also the first day of the week, which makes them a great time to unfocus and refocus. For leaders, this may be the time most suited to spend strategic time with the few kids or teenagers in your circle. Sundays can become the best time to zero in on your relationship with God. If not Sunday, then when is the most logical opportunity to fuel your faith together? Why not go ahead and circle it? Build some time into every week for a community of faith.

JUST REMEMBER WHAT YOU DO THIS WEEK CAN MAKE A DIFFERENCE. BECAUSE WHAT YOU DO THIS WEEK IS CONNECTED TO NEXT WEEK . . . AND THE NEXT . . . AND THE NEXT. AND THE WEEKS ADD UP. THEY HAVE THE POTENTIAL OVER TIME TO GIVE THE KIDS IN YOUR LIFE THE

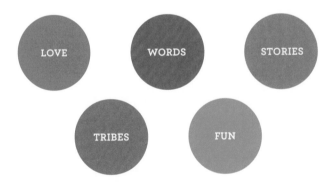

THEY WILL NEED TO BUILD A BETTER FUTURE.

From the Losing Your Marbles story

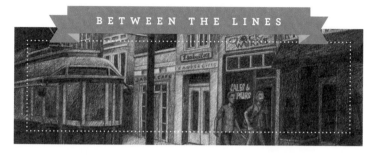

BETWEEN THE LINES

THINK ABOUT	THINK ABOUT
KEN	**LISA**
IF YOU'RE A LEADER	IF YOU'RE A PARENT

Ken leads a group of awkward, misfit zombies—that is, middle-school boys. He knows they need to be connected to a story bigger than themselves. He wants to help them have an authentic faith that stands the tests of time. That's why he has chosen to be present during these transitional years. He could probably do something more exciting with his Sunday afternoon than film middle-schoolers in a cemetery. But Ken's not expecting immediate results or instant change. He's committed to being present in their lives for a critical season. He trusts what can happen to their character and faith over time.

She loves her son Eric. At this point in her teenage son's life, she is feeling what a lot of parents feel. She blinked, and the kid who made her macaroni-covered valentines and went camping under a sheet in her living room has turned into a brooding teenager she hardly recognizes. She shows up at his concert not because late night riverside concerts are her thing, but because it's what Eric loves. Whether she realizes it or not, her presence in his life matters. Eric may be growing up, but he will never grow out of the need for his parents and a relationship with someone who has known him over time.

KNUCKLE DOWN:

Like Ken and Lisa, you have chosen to invest time over time in the lives of a few. Write down their names. Next to each one, write the number of weeks you have left before they graduate or move on to the next phase of life. What are a few things you want to do with them in the time you have left?

THE TIME YOU SPEND THIS WEEK WITH A KID OR TEENAGER MATTERS.

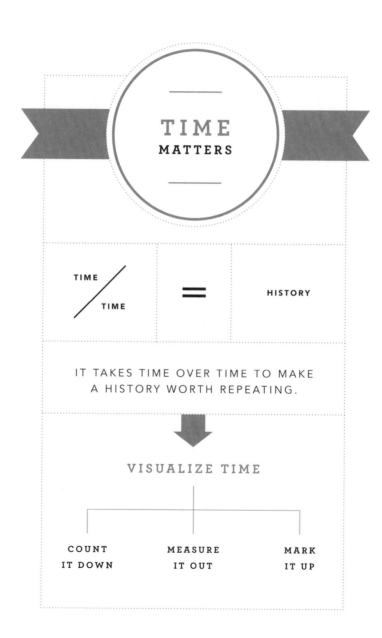

TIME
MATTERS

TIME / TIME = HISTORY

IT TAKES TIME OVER TIME TO MAKE
A HISTORY WORTH REPEATING.

VISUALIZE TIME

COUNT
IT DOWN

MEASURE
IT OUT

MARK
IT UP

LOVE

—————— *over* ——————

TIME

IS THE ONE THING
THAT MATTERS MOST

LOVE

Matters

LOVE

Matters

If you want to know what
kids and teenagers need over time,
love is definitely the best place to start.

Without love, the rest of this book wouldn't make any sense at all.
Actually a lot of things wouldn't make any sense if it weren't for love.

Just take **music** for example.

Without love . . .

There would be no
Whitney, Aretha, Dolly, Madonna, or Lady Gaga.

There would be no
Elvis, Elton, Eagles, Beatles, or Barry White.

Without love . . .

The Blues would be beige.
Country music would only be about beer and tractors.
Rock & Roll would need more guitar solos.
Rap . . . well, that would probably stay the same.

Let's face it.

This world just wouldn't be a good place without love.
It may be the best idea that ever came along.

IF YOU'RE READING THIS BOOK,
YOU PROBABLY BELIEVE IN GOD,
WHICH MEANS YOU ALREADY KNOW
WHO CAME UP WITH THE IDEA
OF LOVE.

IF YOU REALLY THINK ABOUT THAT,
IT EXPLAINS A LOT.
NO WONDER LOVE GETS SO
MUCH PRESS.

God is a pretty good innovator, and He originated the brand.
It's a good thing He didn't copyright it. There would be a lot of people out of a job.

The Bachelor would lose millions of viewers.
No one would listen to Delilah.
Hallmark would go bankrupt.

If you believe love was God's idea, then a lot of things make sense.

For example, maybe you can understand why . . .
a newborn is so dependent on a mother's touch.
a child craves approval from a father.
a teenager looks for belonging.
two people will ~~fall in love~~ hold hands

The point is if love is God's idea, then every person you meet
has been . . .
created to need love.
designed to pursue intimacy.
wired to connect.

SO, LOVE
MATTERS.

Although most of us would agree on that point, it's interesting how
we still have a tendency to go through life acting like love is *not* what
matters most.

You'd think we'd know by now.
Especially those of us who say we believe in God.
But somehow we get so busy trying to matter,
that we forget what actually matters.
Or I should say we forget "Who" matters.

It's kind of like the Pharisees. You remember them, right? They were
religious leaders who believed in God. They actually spent a lot of time
learning what they thought mattered to God.

NO ONE...

| Worked harder at keeping the rules. | Showed up at the temple more consistently. | Prayed longer and harder. | Studied the Scriptures more diligently. |

But they were so busy doing important things they missed the most important thing. Maybe that's why Jesus told them that one thing mattered more than anything else. He was just trying to keep everyone on track.

THERE'S A TENDENCY FOR ANY OF US TO
LOSE FOCUS.
DRIFT AWAY.
MAJOR ON WHAT'S MINOR.

So, Jesus reprioritized in just a few sentences what matters most. He said it like this:

THE GREATEST COMMANDMENT IS TO LOVE THE LORD YOUR GOD WITH ALL OF YOUR MIND, SOUL, AND STRENGTH. BUT THERE'S A SECOND PART TO THIS COMMANDMENT THAT'S JUST AS IMPORTANT AS THE FIRST: LOVE YOUR NEIGHBOR AS YOURSELF.[1]

There it is again. Let me sum it up:
LOVE MATTERS.

Loving God **matters.**
Loving yourself **matters.**
Loving people **matters.**

Actually, the Great Commandment makes several points at once about love.
Loving God helps you love yourself.
Loving God helps you love others.
Loving yourself helps you love God.
Loving yourself helps you love others.
Loving others helps you love God.
Loving others helps you love yourself.

And all are true at the same time.

What a genius idea.
Of course it is.
It came from the One who made you.

Before you get too opinionated about an overemphasis on love,
remember who said it. Just be careful you don't minimize what Jesus
maximized.

Stay focused.

The Beatles may have sung about it,
but Jesus had the idea first.
All you need is love.

> LOVE IS . . .
> the summary for the rest of the commandments.
> the foundation for how we should treat others.
> the mission for every church.
> the filter for how we should see the world.
> the framework for what we say and teach.
> the blueprint for building our lives.
> the reason Jesus came to sacrifice His life for us.

Yep.

If you know the gospel story, you know God used time to prove
something He could only prove over time: His love for us is
unconditional and predictable. You and I can know we matter because
we matter to God.

So, if love matters, the way you love others matters too—especially the
way you love kids.

Have you ever stopped to think that love happens to be the best strategy to help kids know they matter?

Okay. Maybe that's not an original thought.
Let me try another one.

HAVE YOU EVER STOPPED TO THINK THAT

LOVE MATTERS MORE IN THE LIFE OF A KID THAN IT DOES IN THE LIFE OF AN ADULT?

Think about that for a few minutes.

This past year, I (Reggie) had two friends both take their own lives.
One was 23.
One was 48.

The first grew up in a strange cult that pushed her into sex trafficking.
The second grew up in a "Christian home" and wrestled with anorexia.

They both shared a common dilemma:
They didn't know how to love themselves.

They were both smart, attractive, determined people who tried really hard at life.

But something was broken when they were young that stacked the odds against them. I'm not qualified to explain how or why. And it's much more complicated than this chapter can resolve. But here's a point to consider:

KIDS NEED TO LEARN TO LOVE THEMSELVES WHILE THEY'RE KIDS.

Two things give you worth: You were created in God's image. You were redeemed by His Son. Don't get so good at seeing the bad, you forget how to see what someone is worth.

Kids desperately need adults who will love them in a way that will convince them they are worth something. If kids don't feel loved when they are young, they may never love themselves in a healthy way. And if they never learn to love themselves, they may ultimately self-destruct.

So, the way you love kids while they're kids can dramatically affect their futures.

That's why we need more adults to step it up.
It's time to get serious about loving the children around you.

Most research suggests that when it comes to love, the younger the recipient, the more powerful the impact.

When do you actually start creating a sense of worth in a child?
That's simple:
the day they are born.

Most counselors and psychologists agree we should start loving a child as soon as possible. Many of them cite research about brain development that indicates the systems that manage our emotional responses are fundamentally shaped by early experiences in our lives.

Sue Gerhardt is a British psychotherapist who does focused research on emotional health in children. In her book, *Why Love Matters*, she explains the brain systems that manage emotional responses are shaped by early events. Gerhardt says, "Just as the baby's body adapts to a shortage of nutrition, so the brain adapts to inadequate emotional input."[2] Gerhardt builds a case for the importance of love by providing brain scans that show significant physical differences between the brains of children who have been neglected and those who have received normal amounts of affection. She concludes that, "The whole process of developing a social brain and developing a strong sense of self is based on the quality of social attention . . . Basically, humans have to pass on a social brain. The brain (of a child) is built up through actual experiences. What you put in is more or less what you get out."[3]

That's why . . .
Love is like investing—it gains shares.
The sooner you start paying in, the greater the return will be later.
The longer you wait, the less you earn.

SIMPLY PUT:
Deposits in someone's life as a child
will earn more interest.
When you wait until they're adults,
the gains are slower.

My (Reggie) oldest daughter is an artist. When she was a child, she believed every flat surface was a canvas. That included every
wall,
table,
book,
door,
and piece of paper.

She used pencils, pens, markers, chalk, crayons, and paint to leave her mark everywhere. There were constant reminders of her talent all around us, all the time. They were her priceless creations.

I have to be honest. Sometimes, it felt like her art was costing me a lot more than it was worth. I'm not sure I recognized the value of what was happening. If you had asked me then, I would have priced it sentimentally.

But slowly over time, her art evolved from uninteresting smears and scratches to sophisticated, emotional, and intricate paintings. During the past few years, people have paid thousands of dollars for what she creates. Her experiences in life as a child and teenager have begun paying off as an adult.

WHEN YOU START IMAGINING THE FUTURE OF A CHILD, YOU WILL START INVESTING MORE IN THEM NOW.

If loving a child early begins to build a healthy sense of worth, rejecting a child early can do the opposite.

According to the World Health Organization,

"RESEARCH NOW SHOWS THAT MANY CHALLENGES IN ADULT SOCIETY—MENTAL HEALTH PROBLEMS, OBESITY/STUNTING, HEART DISEASE, CRIMINALITY, COMPETENCE IN LITERACY AND NUMERACY—HAVE THEIR ROOTS IN EARLY CHILDHOOD."[4]

This is why children should be a priority in every home, school, and church.
How we love them in their youth will affect how they live as adults.

There is a brief window of time—from birth through adolescence—when what we do in someone's life can matter more than at any other time.

The time you spend every week with
a child
playing,
reading,
talking,
laughing,
and loving is worth it.

It's worth it, because they are worth it.
But again you know that because you
are older and wiser.

So, if you want kids to grow up and know they are worth it, then look for ways to prove it over time.

Kids and teenagers need adults who will show up and be there
Consistently
Patiently
Regardless

They need adults who care enough to discover who they really are and how they are wired.

If you want them to know that love is more than just a "second-hand emotion," they need someone in their lives who will not bolt and run when things get messy.

They need to know that's . . .

HOW LOVE WORKS.

WHAT LOVE DOES.

WHY LOVE MATTERS.

HABIT 2

PROVE IT

*Be physically and
consistently present*

Kids will test you.
If you don't believe that, you probably haven't been around many.

You figure
since you know you love them,
and you tell them you love them,
they should understand you love them.

But instead, their subconscious reaction is:

Prove it.

That's hardly fair.

But in a world where they are constantly being challenged, evaluated, and tested, they often get a mixed message about love and approval.

On the one hand, you might say, "I love you, no matter what." But on the other, kids and teenagers constantly find themselves in experiences where worth is connected to performance.

It's not that you shouldn't affirm them when they . . .
go to the potty "all by myself."
become a star student.
hit a homerun.
earn a paycheck.
get selected for a solo.

But there's also a place for the kind of love that goes beyond performance.
The kind of love that . . .
takes them out for ice cream when they don't make the team.
drives them to *urgent care* when they break an arm.
goes with them to the movies on a Friday evening "just because."
listens sympathetically after their first break-up—and their second, and their third, and their fourth.

If you want kids and teenagers to . . .
have a healthy sense of self-worth,
believe in a Creator who loves them unconditionally,
discover the value of using their lives to love others,
then you may have to get in the business of actually proving that you love them—no matter what.

Author and artist C. JoyBell C. says it this way:

"THEY SAY YOU HAVE TO EARN THE RIGHT TO BE LOVED; NO, LOVE IS UNCONDITIONAL, IF YOU LOVE SOMEONE, THEY DON'T HAVE TO EARN IT. BUT. THE RIGHT TO TELL SOMEONE THAT YOU LOVE THEM? THAT HAS TO BE EARNED. YOU HAVE TO EARN THE RIGHT TO BE BELIEVED."

As parents and leaders, maybe it's time we start earning the right to be believed. It's time that we start using the time we have to get serious about proving our love to the kids who matter most in our lives.

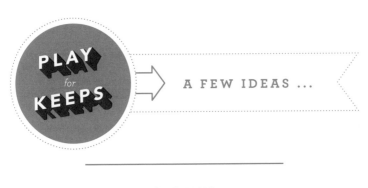

A FEW IDEAS ...

SHOW UP

Okay. That sounds like an understatement. But really, the first way for you to prove to a kid or teenager that you love them is to show up. When we wrote the book *Lead Small* to create a kind of job description for small group leaders, we said the first principle for leading small is to Be Present. That means: you have to show up predictably, randomly, and mentally in the lives of kids. Really, the same is true for anyone who hopes to influence a kid or teenager.

You have to set predictable times when they know you will be present in their lives. If you're a parent, maybe it's every morning at breakfast or every night just before they go to bed. Maybe it's every Tuesday or every Saturday, or just one day out of the week when you have a day off. If you're a leader, maybe it's at a weekly event. Whatever those times are, recognize them, and make every effort to guard them.

You also have to show up for the big events, the non-routine:
the elementary talent show
the middle school band concert
the high school debate tournament

And when you show up for both the predictable and the non-routine—in order for them to count—you have to be fully present in them. The emails, texts, and Instagrams can wait. You are busy giving a child worth. You are proving it.

One more thing about showing up—
Have you ever thought about why you give kids and teenagers rules? Whether you're a leader or a parent, chances are, you have given the kids you are really invested in a few rules. You probably didn't just wake up one morning and decide to tell them to stop driving with one foot out the window—just because you wanted to make their lives boring.

No. You wanted to protect them.
Kids and teenagers need adults who will show up and care enough to give them
rules,
structure,
parameters,
to help keep them safe—emotionally as well as physically.

WHEN YOU SHOW UP TO GIVE KIDS RULES, YOU PROVE YOU CARE.

That's what God did. Think about it. When you read the Old Testament, you don't have to be a biblical scholar to figure out God was in the business of giving rules. I haven't ever personally counted them, but I'm told there are over 600 rules.

It's as if God, the One who created us and understands how we are wired, knew one of the best ways to begin proving His love for us was by showing up for thousands of years to say . . .
Don't eat that.
Don't go there.
You might want to wash that first.

It wasn't the only way He proved His love. But it was one of the first.

KNOW THEM

Knowing a kid or a teenager isn't like knowing the quadratic formula. You learn it once, and it pretty much stays the same. Kids are growing, changing, evolving beings. In order to know them, you have to create spaces in your week to listen. Listen to what they are saying. Listen to what they're not saying. Learn to look for changes in their moods or changes in their activities. If you want to prove to a kid or teenager you really care about them, you need to develop the practice of continually getting to know them.

I (Reggie) learned this the hard way as a parent when I made the mistake of saying to my then-fifth-grade daughter: "I'm your father. Of course I know you." It was in the middle of a conversation, and I probably said it without really thinking. But I wasn't prepared for her response: "No, you don't. You don't know anything about me." She proceeded to give me a pop quiz on everything from her favorite actor to her favorite color. And I remember thinking, *She's going to literally pass or fail me as a father based on my answers to this quiz.*

I LEARNED THAT DAY THERE ARE THREE CATEGORIES OF
INFORMATION FOR ANY LEADER OR PARENT:

**The things we're
supposed to know
that no one tells us.**

**The things we're
supposed to know,
but that can change
at any minute
because they have
a right to
change them.**

**The things we're
not supposed to
know because they
think it's none of
our business.**

Sometimes it's hard to know what falls into each category. But the
stakes are too high not to make knowing them a priority. Set aside
unstructured time to pay attention to what they are saying and how
they are saying it. Spend time over time discovering and re-discovering
the things that make them uniquely who they are.

Really knowing a kid or a teenager will help prove to them their worth.
It requires listening, but it's also more than listening. That's why we will
give you practical ideas in each section of this book that will help you
begin to know them more.

One last thing about knowing them—
When it comes to showing up and creating rules, you will be infinitely
better at creating the rules when you understand the one you are
creating rules for. Okay, I said it. Let's move on to our last idea.

NEVER RUN AWAY

Most of you aren't planning to pack up a duffle bag, walk out the door, and never turn around. But there are times, for many of us, when we (unintentionally) disengage emotionally.

There will come a time in every kid's life when things get messy. Maybe they get sick. Maybe they become sad or hurt emotionally. Maybe they suffer a natural consequence to a decision they made. These aren't the kind of circumstances you create, and you certainly can't change them—even though you might want to. But how you respond in these critical moments will forever impact your relationship. And it will affect the way they respond to and interpret their situations.

Remember when we were talking about rules? It's interesting when you read the Bible and watch how God interacted with the Israelites in the Old Testament. He showed up. He gave them rules. And then they broke the rules, over and over and over again.

Maybe rules were made knowing they would be broken.
It's not that rules weren't made to be followed. I'm sure if we all followed every rule, there would be less anger, pain, and violence. When a rule is broken, it creates a unique opportunity to prove love.

In other words, you have an opportunity as a parent or as a leader to show up in the life of a kid or teenager to give them rules that will help keep them safe physically and emotionally. But when they break a rule (and at some point they will), and you show up anyway, you communicate unconditional love.

That's what God did.
He gave the rules.
We broke them.
He showed up anyway.

It doesn't mean that there won't be consequences. It doesn't mean that there's no place for correction or instruction. Of course, we want to help kids and teenagers learn from their experiences and make wise choices in the future. But it does mean that you should never punish them relationally. Regardless of what they've done, you still have the opportunity to show up to prove . . .
you aren't going anywhere.
they still matter
you will see them through the mess.

IT'S REALLY PRETTY SIMPLE. WHEN WE SHOW UP AND MAKE RULES, WE PROVE TO THEM WE CARE. WHEN THEY BREAK THE RULES AND WE SHOW UP ANYWAY, WE PROVE TO THEM WE STILL CARE. WE PROVE TO THEM THEY HAVE WORTH, AND WE ARE COMMITTED TO THEM EVEN WHEN IT'S DIFFICULT, INCONVENIENT, AND MESSY.

A few years ago, we had the privilege of meeting with education reformer Geoffrey Canada about children who grow up in disadvantaged environments. Canada is an education reformer who grew up in the South Bronx, went to Harvard graduate school, and came back to Harlem as the president and CEO of the Harlem Children's Zone. He has dedicated his life to giving kids a better chance by helping them graduate high school and get into college.

In a conversation with Geoffrey, he made an interesting observation about the kids in Harlem. He said the reason so many of these kids don't believe in God is because they've never seen adults who are God-like.

What he was saying was simple. In order to believe in a good and creative God who loves them in spite of their mistakes and their mess, kids and teenagers need adults who will do the same. They need adults who can demonstrate to them over time that they matter and have a value far greater than what can be measured by their performance.

THEY NEED PARENTS AND LEADERS LIKE YOU

who will be present in their lives
in order to know them,
and never run away,
so they will know how much they're worth.

From the Losing Your Marbles story

BETWEEN THE LINES

THINK ABOUT

SIMON

Simon's a weird kid. He plays marbles, and for a twelve-year-old who has grown up without a father, he's exceptionally levelheaded. Seriously, how many middle-schoolers do *you* know like Simon? Of course, this story only gives us a glimpse into one week of his life. There are probably a lot of other sides to Simon, too.

Nevertheless, Simon has gumption. He's a spirited, gutsy, resourceful kid with enough confidence to take on the top dogs of his middle school single-handedly. Okay, maybe not single-handedly. But he takes them on nonetheless. Why?

Simon has a healthy sense of self-worth.

From the Losing Your Marbles story

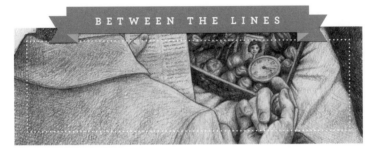

BETWEEN THE LINES

MAYBE THAT'S WHY . . .

He is unsusceptible to Nick's schemes. He has the confidence to think clearly and not be pushed around.

He understands how to care for someone unselfishly. He goes to great lengths not only to keep Max out of trouble, but to help Max figure out a better way to fit in at a new school.

He has the courage to open up to Eric. Simon's vulnerability with Eric helps Eric begin to discover what it really means to love other people.

Simon may seem like a rare kid with a healthy perspective about what matters, but did you notice something? Simon wouldn't be Simon if it weren't for some other key people in his life. Without the influence and love of his mother, Diane, and his small group leader, Ken, and even his next-door neighbor and drum instructor, Eric, Simon probably wouldn't be the heroic kid that he is.

In other words, Simon knows that he's worth something because certain adults in his life have shown up consistently, over time, to prove to him that he's worth loving. And because he knows that he's worth loving, he is, in turn, able to demonstrate love to the people around him.

KNUCKLE DOWN:

Who are the people who have loved you over time and proved to you that you matter? List a few things they did to prove it to you.

WHAT YOU DO THIS WEEK TO LOVE A KID OR TEENAGER MATTERS.

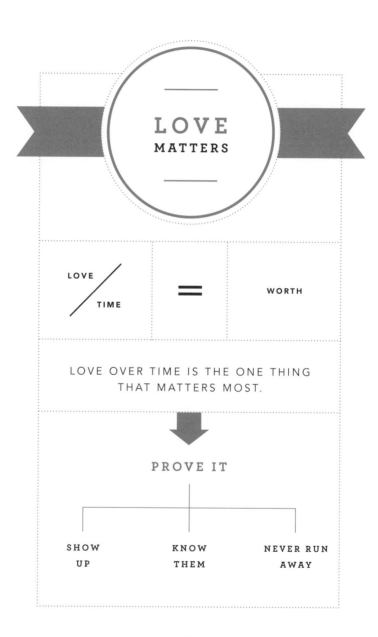

LOVE
MATTERS

$$\frac{LOVE}{TIME} = WORTH$$

LOVE OVER TIME IS THE ONE THING
THAT MATTERS MOST.

PROVE IT

SHOW
UP

KNOW
THEM

NEVER RUN
AWAY

WORDS

over

TIME

CAN IMPACT SOMEONE'S DIRECTION IN LIFE

WORDS

Matter

WORDS

Matter

If you want to help kids and teenagers
know they are loved over time,
tell them, "**I LOVE YOU.**"

Okay. Now that we have gotten the most obvious, true, and
predictable idea out of the way, let's talk a little more about words. [1]

We all have a tendency to underestimate the weight of our words—
especially as it relates to the kids and teenagers we care about.

If you've ever traveled to a place with a language different from your
own, you know that words matter.

Maybe you've accidently . . .
confused *jamon* with *jabon* and ordered a soap sandwich.
mistaken *ocas* for *ojos* and sought medical attention for your
inflamed geese.
forgotten the gender for *busto* and asked the post office clerk for a
corset (*busta*).

But there's more to a language than sorting out confusing homonyms.

In Pormpuraaw, a remote aboriginal community in Australia, words
like "right," "left," "in front of," or "behind" don't exist. Instead, the
people use cardinal directions:

"Please hand me the plate west of your cup."
"You may sit in the seat to my east."
"There's an ant on your southwest leg."

If you want to greet someone, you might ask, "Where are you going?" and they might answer, "A long way to the south-southwest. How about you?"[2]

 WHAT'S THE POINT?

In order to say anything in Kuuk Thaayorer, you have to be spatially oriented. If you aren't, you literally can't even say "Hello" properly. That means speakers of Kuuk Thaayorer are remarkably good at navigation, even in unfamiliar landscapes.[3]

They are good at navigation
because they constantly think about direction.

They think about direction
because they use directional words.

SIMPLY PUT:
THE WORDS THEY USE
IMPACT THE WAY
THEY THINK.

The same is true not only for different languages, but for any academic field of study.
Whether you want to learn
anthropology,
psychology,
herbology,
theology, or
mechanical engineering,
you will have to learn some new words.

**WITHOUT THE RIGHT WORDS,
YOU CAN'T UNDERSTAND
THE CONCEPTS.**

The way you see the world is shaped by the words you use to express what you see.
You are able to see what you know how to say.

Research has actually shown, in order to . . .
think a thought,
paint a picture,
work a math problem,
you need words.

Without words—the simplest tools of communication—people are limited.

So, if words allow us to
think,
see,
interpret,
then they must be a big deal to God.

AFTER ALL, EVERYTHING STARTED WITH A WORD.

God spoke and it came into being.
God created with words.

The first words we know about were God's:

"LET THERE BE LIGHT."

Maybe it's no accident that
words have been helping us see ever since.

God used words to create a world out of nothing. Theologians use the phrase *ex nihilo* to distinguish this kind of "creation" from anything else that is simply made using existing elements.

GOD'S WORDS HAVE POWER.

But God didn't reserve the power of words only for Himself.
Adam didn't get to create *ex nihilo*, but he did get to name the animals.

Adam decided,
"This one is a slug."
"That's a butterfly."

God gave Adam the creative power to name something.
He shared with humanity the incredible ability to . . .
give meaning,
define attributes,
AND SHAPE PERCEPTIONS OF THE CREATED WORLD.

By sharing the power of words, by giving us the gift of communication,
God gave us a tremendous responsibility.

It's easy to take words for granted.
We use them every day.

**But the words we use not only affect what we see,
they affect how we influence others to see.**

As a parent or leader, you decide what words you will give to the kids
and teenagers in your life. But remember, like all things with power,
words have the potential to do as much damage as they do good.

> They can be used to . . .
> love or scorn.
> encourage or tear down.
> illuminate or shut out.

What you say probably has more of an impact than you think it does. Maybe that's why James warns us words are like a bridle on a horse or a rudder on a ship.

Words are small things, but they have tremendous **influence.**
They can impact someone's direction.

That's why the words you give to a kid or teenager this week matter.
Your words aren't just
empty.
overused.
meaningless.

Every time you speak, you are reinforcing or expanding
their vocabulary.
You are giving them words. Words that will shape . . .
how they see the world.
how they see themselves.
how they think about God.

Your words will help them imagine and understand the things they can't see so they can keep moving in a good direction.

When you don't know something, you usually don't know you
don't know.
Until recently I didn't know I couldn't navigate like the Aborigines.
Everything in my world is left or right. That's all I have.
But I do get lost pretty easily.

In the same way, the kids and teenagers in your world probably don't know the words they need from you. But you have a unique opportunity to give them words over time that will help them
Reason
Win
Believe

Words over time help kids **REASON.**

It's really not complicated to understand.
You need words to think.

So, the more words you have, the more . . .
ideas you can ideate.
intuition you can intuit.
thoughts you can think.

If you want kids to be able to reason,
they need words.

 DID YOU KNOW ONE OF THE GREATEST INDICATORS OF A CHILD'S FUTURE SUCCESS IS VOCABULARY?

MAYBE THAT'S WHY . . .
- "The U.S. Military's Armed Forces Qualification Test gives twice as much weight to verbal scores as to math scores."[4]
- The SAT is weighted toward verbal abilities two to one.

They are acting on the belief that the greater your variety of words, the greater your scope of thinking.

How effective would you be if you were a . . .
musician with only two notes?
chef with only three ingredients?
mechanic with only one tool?

THE TRUTH IS
KIDS NEED TO INCREASE
THEIR VOCABULARY
IN ORDER TO BE
MORE SUCCESSFUL.

If you want to help a kid or teenager be an
innovator,
problem solver,
learner,
then give them words.

Because if they never expand their vocabulary,
they will grow up to be
limited,
stuck,
dependent.

Words over time help kids **WIN**.

If words in general help us think, problem-solve, and learn
new concepts, a few select words have the ability to shape the way we
Feel
Hope
Dream

IF YOU WANT A KID TO KNOW THEY
MATTER, THEN IT MATTERS WHAT
WORDS YOU USE WHEN YOU TALK
TO THEM AND **ABOUT** THEM

THE WORDS YOU USE CAN SET
THEM UP TO FEEL

SIGNIFICANT • VALUED • UNIQUE

Or the words you use can unintentionally limit them, box them in, and
make them feel trapped.

When I (Kristen) was a high school English teacher, I had one of those experiences that makes teaching one of the greatest professions on the planet. (I may be biased.) In my third-period class, I had a student with some learning disabilities. He was quiet, unsocial, and on a number of medications. He always kept his head down and never participated. Then one day, he turned in a story I was *sure* he had plagiarized. This story was so good, so well-written, I just knew it couldn't be his work.

After hours of investigating, I discovered that it *was* his writing.

So I did what any teacher would have done.
I TOLD HIM HE WAS A GOOD WRITER.

The next thing I knew, he was bringing me stories after school—unassigned—just to get feedback. He took the initiative to launch a writers' club at the school. He started getting better grades. He smiled more. He became more socially connected. Now he's a *New York Times* best-selling author.

Okay, he's not a best-selling author . . . that I know of.
But when he started writing, he discovered something about his potential.
It changed the way he saw himself.
It moved him in a better direction.

For my part, it was only a few simple words.
They didn't feel significant at the time.
I assumed he already knew he was a good writer.
I figured someone else must have told him.

But that one conversation,
those few words,
MADE A HUGE IMPACT.

As a parent or leader, you might not get many of those stories. You rarely know the impact of your own words. You won't often hear things like . . .

"Wow, I never thought about it that way."

"Thanks, Mom. Your words made me feel so loved."

"When you said that, it really changed how I think about . . . "

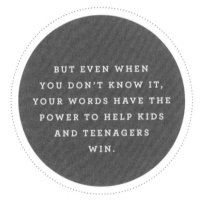

BUT EVEN WHEN YOU DON'T KNOW IT, YOUR WORDS HAVE THE POWER TO HELP KIDS AND TEENAGERS WIN.

Words over time help kids **BELIEVE.**

Everything you know about God, you know through words.

Okay, maybe that's hyperbole—*maybe*.

But our theology is expressed in words.

You have never seen

Redemption

Justification

Kenosis

> Did you look it up? Good. See, even you can discover something about God by expanding your vocabulary.

KIDS AND TEENAGERS NEED
THEOLOGICAL WORDS IN ORDER TO
UNDERSTAND CERTAIN ASPECTS OF
GOD'S NATURE. THAT'S WHY THE
WORDS YOU GIVE THEM MATTER WHEN
IT COMES TO FAITH.

Your
analogies,
adjectives,
and questions
will shape what they think about when they think about God.

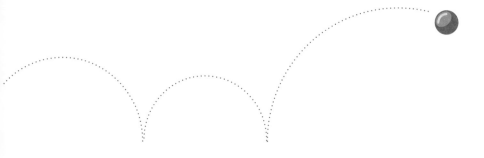

If you grew up without a concept of God, you may be tempted to shut down or feel defeated right now. Maybe you're asking yourself, *How can I pass on a theological vocabulary if I don't even know any theological words?*

Actually, you may be in a better place than the rest of us.
For some of us, there are words that may have been overused or abused when we were forming our thoughts about God and faith.

As a leader or a parent, regardless of your background, you have an opportunity to rediscover old words and to look for new and relevant ways to explain ancient and timeless concepts.

If you want to pass on a spiritual history,
give the kids and teenagers in your life spiritual words.

When you give a kid a word,
you open them up to new possibilities.

MAYBE THAT'S WHY GOD GAVE US WORDS. SO WE
COULD SHARE THEM OVER TIME TO . . .

COMMUNICATE LOVE.

BUILD EACH OTHER UP.

MOVE US IN A BETTER DIRECTION.

HABIT 3

EXPAND YOUR
VOCABULARY

*Learn the words
they need to hear*

When you hang around kids and teenagers,
you will find yourself saying some pretty remarkable things.

"Don't sit on your brother's face."
"You're wrong, a gorilla would totally destroy a bear in a fight."
"Can you use your big-kid voice, and ask nicely with a happy heart?"

If you say that last one to a group of eleventh-grade guys, you are likely
to get some pretty interesting looks. That's not because it's a bad phrase.
It's just that it's not a good phrase for that particular season of life.

WORDS ARE ALWAYS CHANGING.

The words you use with preschoolers aren't the same words you will use
with an elementary-school kid. And the words you use for a fifth-grader will
look distinctly different than the words you use with an eleventh-grader.

There are new words for every season of life.

If you're a leader who has worked with fifth-graders for fifteen years,
maybe you think you have an out on this one. Think again. Words don't
only change as kids get older, they change with time. Culture changes.
With the release of every new movie, every new music group, every
new TV show, new words trickle through our conversations. Some stick
around for longer than others. But language is always changing.

That means whether you're a parent or a leader, you will never know all
the words. Instead, you will constantly be learning.

YOU WILL ALWAYS NEED TO EXPAND YOUR VOCABULARY.

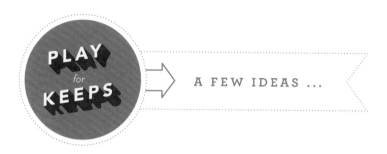

A FEW IDEAS ...

LEARN ANOTHER LANGUAGE

If you're like me, the idea of learning another language is terrifying. Hands down, Spanish was the hardest class of my life. I'd rather do just about anything than parse another verb. But don't worry. We aren't suggesting you need to run out and buy Rosetta Stone.®

But, like we said—if you are going to expand your vocabulary so you can give kids the rational, emotional, and theological words they need, you *will* constantly be learning another language.

You need to learn a faith language to help them believe.
You need to learn an emotional language so you can help them win.
You need to learn more language so you can help them reason.

Here's the good news: Just like when you learn to speak another language, you don't have to do it alone. Find a teacher or a coach—someone who is fluent in the words you need. Look for someone who is an expert in what you need to know.

Maybe they are . . .
an educator who works with a specific age group.
a leader who has a way of describing concepts of faith.
a parent of older kids who has had time to reflect on a particular season
of life.

If you don't personally know someone who would be a great
language coach, that's okay. People write books for a reason. Take a
trip to your local bookstore or get online and do a little research. You
can probably find
an author,
a researcher,
a blogger,
or some other expert who can help you expand your vocabulary so you
can have a lasting impact.

> THE POINT IS DISCOVER WHO YOU WANT TO LISTEN TO, SO YOU
> WILL HAVE THE WORDS YOU REALLY NEED WHEN YOU NEED
> THEM MOST.

WEIGH WHAT YOU SAY

Did you know that, on average, people say 10,123 words per day?
That's a lot of words. If you are a parent or leader with teens, the
number you hear from them may be slightly less.
"Not much,"
"Goin' out,"
"Sure," only go so far in the daily total.

But within those 10,123 words, some words count more than others. And those are the words you weigh. Those are the ones to which you give special attention.

They might be the words you say when a kid . . .
asks you a question you weren't expecting.
experiences a significant milestone transition.
opens up about a situation you didn't see coming.
makes a poor decision.

Or they might be words that just happen . . .
over breakfast,
standing in the hall,
or in the car.

Whenever you happen to say them, here are four ways you can weigh the words that matter most.

WRITE IT OUT

If you aren't sure what you want to say, take the time to write it. You think about your words differently when you write them down. You can pick the right words, arrange them in just the right order, and practice saying what you really want to say before you have to say it.

MAKE IT SPECIFIC

The words that count most are the words we know have been created specifically for us. The reason my conversation with the student I mentioned earlier was so meaningful for him wasn't because I told him he was a good writer. It was because he *is* a good writer, and I told him. It was specific *for* him. Every kid, every teenager, needs to hear a specific compliment from someone who knows them best. They need for you to use words that shine a light on the things they do well. They need for you to catch them doing something right.

If you are looking for a place to start making it specific, try completing the following phrases as they relate to the kids and teenagers in your life:

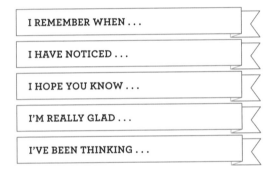

I REMEMBER WHEN . . .

I HAVE NOTICED . . .

I HOPE YOU KNOW . . .

I'M REALLY GLAD . . .

I'VE BEEN THINKING . . .

Maybe you can even make it a practice to write short notes—two or three sentences—that begin with these phrases. If you're a parent, put the note in a kid's lunch, on the nightstand, under the wiper blades of your teenager's car. If you're a leader, send it through the mail, write it in a text, or use whatever social media platform they are on. Get creative about how you personalize it, so they will have regular reminders over time that you know and love them.

REMEMBER THE BASICS

This might be the easiest thing you can put into practice. It may even seem like a contradiction to everything else we have said so far. But there are some common phrases every kid and teenager needs to hear from the adults who know and love them. They don't have to be learned from a teacher or a coach. They don't change as a kid gets older. You don't even have to do much to personalize them. Just use them. And use them more than once.

Are you wondering what the phrases are?
HERE'S AN INCOMPLETE LIST TO GET YOU STARTED:

"THANK YOU."
"I LOVE YOU."
"I'M SORRY."
"I DON'T KNOW, BUT WE CAN FIND OUT."
"IT'S OKAY, I'VE MADE MISTAKES TOO."
"I'M HERE FOR YOU."
"I BELIEVE IN YOU."
"YOU DID IT!"
"I'M PROUD OF YOU."
"I TRUST YOU."
"I'M LISTENING."
"I LOVE SPENDING TIME WITH YOU."
"KEEP TRYING."
"YOU CAN DO IT."

You can add more as you think of them.

LET THEM TALK

The words you give a kid or teenager have the potential to welcome
a conversation or shut one down. Don't miss that. Your words matter
when it comes to prompting them to share words with you—and they
need to share words with you. Think about the people in your life to

whom you feel safe talking. Chances are, they have communicated to you over time that they enjoy hearing from you—even when it might be
Inconvenient
Unplanned
Informal

Some of the best ways to weigh your words
are to practice asking good questions,
listening well, and developing conversation skills.

You'll find that when you

STAY FASCINATED,
UNDER-REACT,
VALUE WAIT TIME,
and **WELCOME INTERRUPTIONS,**

you may begin to hear more from the kids and teenagers in your life. That's good. Because as much as your words matter, you shouldn't be the only one talking.

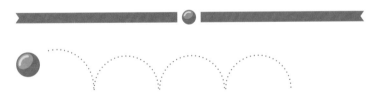

RECYCLE BIG IDEAS

What are the phrases you remember most? When you were growing up, there were probably some core values that were transferred to you through words. But chances are, you don't remember the things someone only said once. You remember the things someone said to you repeatedly over time.

So, as a parent or leader, what do you want those phrases to be? What are the core ideas you want the kids and teenagers in your life to walk away and remember?

Before you pull out your iPad and start writing down your list, let me stop you for a minute. What if I told you that you might not have to come up with all the phrases yourself? I'm not saying you can't. You might have some genius phrases you know immediately need to become a part of your vocabulary.

But here's something you might not have considered before:

There are people who have dedicated their professional career to creating phrases worth repeating in the life of a child. That's why if you're on a church staff, it's a good idea to choose a curriculum that will give you a strong starting point. If you are a parent or volunteer leader, maybe you need to take the time to understand the curriculum and message your church has adopted.

What if all you had to do in order to recycle big ideas was to steal what some smart people around you are already saying?

THERE'S ACTUALLY AN ADDED BONUS
TO BORROWING PHRASES. NOT ONLY DO
YOU SAVE YOURSELF SOME TIME, YOU
ALSO INCREASE THE ODDS YOU WILL BE
HEARD. AS A LEADER OR PARENT, WHEN
YOU BEGIN TO SAY THE SAME THING IN
THE SAME WAY SOMEONE ELSE
IS SAYING IT, YOU HAVE A
GREATER IMPACT.

Once you identify core values and ideas worth recycling, there are a few ways you can make those ideas stick:

HAVE A MONTHLY FOCUS

Choose one idea to repeat often over a short period of time.

INCORPORATE IT INTO YOUR "EVERYDAY"

Use the routine moments of life to highlight the ideas that are most significant.

SAY IT THE SAME WAY

When you say the same thing the same way, it makes it memorable. But over time, it can become white noise. So you should also . . .

SAY IT IN A NEW WAY

When you hear something in a new way, sometimes it helps you reframe the thought and understand it at a deeper level.

HAVE SOMEONE ELSE SAY IT

Again, this is why we wrote the book to parents and leaders alike. When you get on the same page to say the same thing, you have the potential to make a greater impact in the life of a kid or teenager.

REMEMBER:
YOU ARE MAKING HISTORY IN THE
LIVES OF KIDS AND TEENAGERS. THIS
WEEK, YOUR WORDS HAVE INCREDIBLE
POTENTIAL TO . . .

TURN ON A LIGHT.
HELP SOMEONE SEE.

That's why you do what you do.
You understand the importance of words over time.
You know a few simple words can have a lasting influence.

So, when you say something this week,
say it so it matters,
and say it so someone
knows they matter.

A few words can make a big difference in the direction of someone's life.

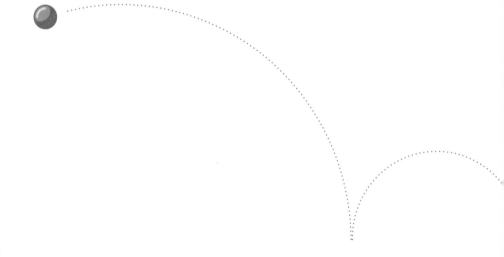

From the Losing Your Marbles story

BETWEEN THE LINES

THINK ABOUT

MARCUS

Marcus works with words. He's a writer who carries around a physical dictionary *and* thesaurus. Who does that anymore? And yet, when it comes to the words he really needs to communicate with his son, Eric, he has a hard time knowing what to say.

He believes his son is a good kid.
He wants to inspire Eric to make something of himself.
He's proud of his son's talent.

But Eric doesn't keep a mental catalog of Marcus' good intentions. Instead, Eric remembers his father's words:

"You don't have an ounce of motivation."
"You're irrational."
"Idealistic."
"You're going nowhere."

From the Losing Your Marbles story

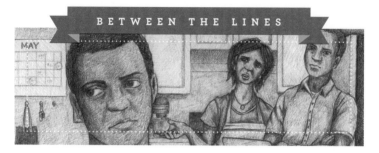

BETWEEN THE LINES

Like so many parents and leaders, Marcus struggles to turn his intentions into words that can help move Eric in a better direction. In his rush to complete a deadline at work, he absent-mindedly says things that don't fully communicate what he wants to say.

But what if Marcus really understood the impact his words have on Eric? What if he began to view his words as a gift that, over time, could ultimately impact the direction of his son's life?

Maybe then Marcus would give the words that he says to his son the kind of study and attention he gives the words he writes about Memphian real estate. Okay, maybe that's harsh. But Marcus is a fictional character; he can handle the criticism.

KNUCKLE DOWN:

Don't make Marcus' mistake. Think about what you need to say. What are a few of the most important messages you want to communicate over time to the kids in your circle of influence?

EXPAND YOUR
VOCABULARY

THE WORDS **YOU GIVE A KID OR TEENAGER THIS WEEK MATTER.**

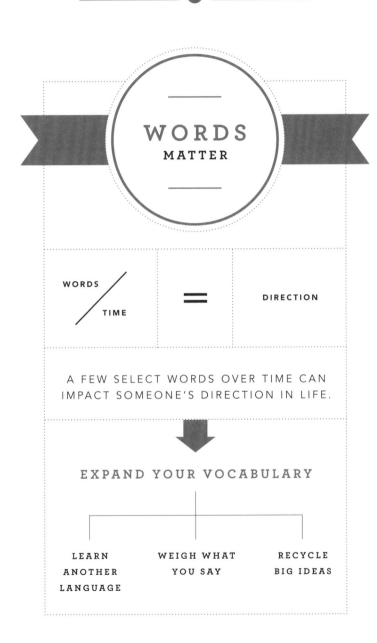

WORDS
MATTER

$$\frac{\text{WORDS}}{\text{TIME}} = \text{DIRECTION}$$

A FEW SELECT WORDS OVER TIME CAN IMPACT SOMEONE'S DIRECTION IN LIFE.

EXPAND YOUR VOCABULARY

| LEARN ANOTHER LANGUAGE | WEIGH WHAT YOU SAY | RECYCLE BIG IDEAS |

STORIES

TIME

STORIES

over

TIME

MOVE US TO IMAGINE A
WORLD BEYOND OURSELVES

STORIES

Matter

STORIES

Matter

Ask any
teacher,
marketer,
politician,
journalist,
or photographer.

STORY IS EVERYTHING.

And if your audience includes children or teenagers,
stories are even more important.

Have you ever wondered what grandparents, fiction, and the Bible
have in common? Probably not. Why would you? But if you think about
it, they represent at least three different kinds of stories that shape a
child's perspective about the world.

Don't get worried.
We don't think the Bible is fiction
or that fiction is more important than the Bible.

We just believe kids and teenagers need stories from grandparents, fiction, *and* the Bible to build the kind of history they really need.

Think about it.

KIDS NEED STORIES FROM GRANDPARENTS.

Okay. It may not be possible for every kid to have or know a biological grandparent. But children at least need figurative grandparents— influences in their lives who are
older adults,
guardians,
aunts and uncles,
or simply friends of the family who have been around long enough to connect kids to meaningful stories about their parents or heritage.

Without personal and family stories, kids miss out on having the kind of *relational* history that fuels a healthy perspective about their identity.

KIDS NEED FICTIONAL STORIES.

Some Christians may get nervous about this statement.
But instead of having a Harry Potter, Hunger Games, or
Santa Claus debate, let's at least agree on one thing:
God seems to like fiction.

STORIES / TIME

On the one hand, the Bible is true. But at the same time, it also contains a lot of fiction. Fiction was the primary way Jesus amplified truth. He taught in parables because sometimes the best way to clarify a truth is to tell a story.

Without fiction, kids could miss part of the *cultural* history they need to connect with a wider community and develop values.

KIDS NEED BIBLE STORIES.

We decided to put this at the bottom of our list for a reason—
Not because it's less important, but actually because it is
more important.

The Bible isn't a book.
It's actually a library of 66 books, written by 40 different authors over 1,600 years. They were all very different people ranging from nomads to kings, from priests to fishermen. Yet all of its stories connect to tell one story about God and His love for us through time.

Without the Bible, kids and teenagers could grow up and fail to connect the great mysteries of the universe with a creative and loving God. They would miss out on the kind of *spiritual* history that is foundational to faith.

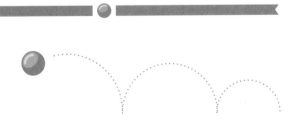

That's why stories matter.
They provide kids with the relational, cultural, and spiritual context to shape their perspectives about
God
Faith
Values
Life

So, what does that have to do with you?
As leaders and parents, you are
storytellers,
producers,
librarians,
or maybe even photojournalists.
You should always be looking for the next story to help them have a richer history, because . . .

STORIES OVER TIME SHAPE
SOMEONE'S PERSPECTIVE.

STORIES ARE JUST ANOTHER ONE OF
GOD'S BRILLIANT IDEAS TO CONNECT
US TO WHAT REALLY MATTERS.

If God created TIME as a platform to prove He LOVES us unconditionally, then maybe He designed STORIES so that collectively, over time, they could give us a deeper perspective about His universal principles and truths.

To put it another way, God fashioned the human brain so it would connect to story. Then, He crafted an original script that would continue to fascinate humans. Then, He designed humans with the creative talent to craft intriguing stories.
(That has to be more than just coincidence.)

Experts have analyzed, theorized, and evangelized about the power of story. Everyone seems to agree. It's as if our minds are hardwired to engage in the way information fits together in the context of a narrative.

One specialist in this area puts it this way:

"IN THE LAST 15 YEARS WE HAVE DEVELOPED THE BRAIN IMAGING TECHNOLOGIES THAT HELP US SHED LIGHT ON WHAT IT MEANS TO 'GET LOST' IN A GOOD STORY. STUDIES ARE SUGGESTING THAT, WHEN READING, LISTENING, OR WATCHING A GOOD STORY, WE ACTIVATE BRAIN REGIONS USED TO PROCESS THE EXPERIENCE AS IF IT WERE OUR OWN. IN OTHER WORDS, WE ARE WIRED FOR STORIES."[1]

If you ever need a little more proof that God exists, consider the
magical,
mystical,
imaginative,
compelling way
kids, teenagers—and everyone else for that matter—connect to stories.

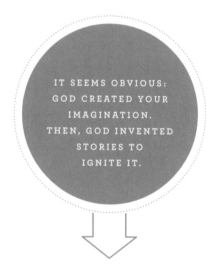

IT SEEMS OBVIOUS:
GOD CREATED YOUR
IMAGINATION.
THEN, GOD INVENTED
STORIES TO
IGNITE IT.

**DON'T UNDERESTIMATE THE POTENTIAL OF
YOUR GOD-GIVEN IMAGINATION.**

Have you ever considered that without imagination, you can't . . .
see past what you already know?
care how someone else feels?
hope beyond your present situation?

J.K. Rowling says, "Imagination is not only the uniquely human capacity to envision that which is not. . . . In its arguably most transformative and revelatory capacity, it is the power that enables us to empathize with humans whose experiences we have never shared. Unlike any other creature on this planet, humans can learn and understand, without having experienced. They can think themselves into other people's places."[2]

That's what the gift of imagination and story does for a child or teenager.

It enables them to think their way into other people's lives.

It compels them to feel the sentiments of other people's emotions.

It invites them to venture into other people's places.

Maybe that's why research actually indicates the more stories you read to a child over time, the greater their empathy.[3] Because stories have the potential to make you feel what someone else feels.

Stories can collectively work to build a child's
emotional,
relational,
and moral intelligence.

Think about what happens when a child imagines . . .
fighting Smaug, the dragon, with Bilbo on the Lonely Mountain.
joining Annemarie in the Danish Resistance during WWII.
traveling with Lucy through a mysterious wardrobe into a frozen land.

THEY SEE MORE.
THEY CARE MORE.
THEY HOPE MORE.

That's what imagination does.
It affects our emotions and intuition.

That same imagination can also help a child embrace complex truths and realities related to stories of faith.

A child has to imagine . . .
the power of what happened when God created the world.
the voice of God to Moses from a burning bush.
the miracles Jesus performed as He traveled the ancient cities.
the majesty of a heavenly dwelling place.

It's as if God gave us an imagination so we could imagine the unimaginable. And stories become the spark that ignites our creative senses and emotions. Stories move us. And stories have the potential to stretch our perspectives about God. Maybe that's why Jesus was such a master at spinning parables to teach people about the character of God.

**CAN YOU IMAGINE
THE ONE WHO FASHIONED YOUR IMAGINATION
TO CONNECT TO STORY,**

CRAFTING STORIES TO ACTUALLY TELL YOU?

True, He had an advantage over the average storyteller.
I wonder if that's why His stories are so
Timeless
Powerful
Life-changing

Jesus said, "Let me tell you a story so you can get a glimpse of God's
character. He's like . . .
a father with a rebellious son.
a rich man who goes on a journey and leaves his estate in the hands of
his servants.
a bridegroom throwing an incredible wedding party."

Then Jesus put *us* in those stories, too.
He said we are like . . .
the casual hiker who stumbles across an incredible pearl in the middle
of a field.
the woman who badgers and pleads with an unjust judge until he
gives in.
the builder furrowing his brow as he decides between two plots of land:
one rough and underlain with rock, the other idyllic and sandy.

> JESUS APPEALED TO THE IMAGINATION AND INVITED US
> INTO THE ACTION.
> AS LEADERS AND PARENTS, WE WOULD BE SMART TO DO
> THE SAME.

THE STORIES YOU TELL MATTER.
YOU ARE INVITING KIDS AND TEENAGERS INTO A BIGGER
NARRATIVE—ONE WHERE THEY HAVE BEEN DESIGNED TO
PLAY A SIGNIFICANT ROLE.

WHY DO YOU THINK . . .

Luke	**Frodo** in *Lord*	**Aslan** in *The*	and a boy
Skywalker in	*of the Rings,*	*Chronicles of*	named **Harry**
Star Wars,		*Narnia,*	

have such an appeal to the hearts of kids?

BECAUSE THEY REMIND US OF . . .

the **struggle**	the **existence** of a	the **potential** to be
between good	supernatural and	personally restored
and evil.	miraculous power.	and transformed.

Why do you think the same themes are recycled so many times?

**MAYBE IT'S SIMPLY BECAUSE THE IDEA OF
STORY ORIGINATED WITH GOD.**

If every story was written by an author who is created in God's image, maybe that's the reason so many reflect His ancient narrative.

NO WONDER STORIES INSPIRE US.
NO WONDER STORIES INCITE FAITH.
NO WONDER STORIES GIVE US HOPE.

Isn't that the kind of perspective you want kids and teenagers to have about this world?
Don't you want them to know life's connected to a bigger story where God is the author?

A bigger story perspective . . .
prepares them to face whatever happens.
compels them to take risks and do something significant.
moves them to keep believing that good will ultimately win.

Life will be hard.
It will be harder for some than for others.
The only guarantee in everyone's story is there will be conflict.

That's why everybody loves a good story.
You latch onto someone who is going against the odds.
You identify with their struggle to push through.

Did you know the script for Harry Potter was written during J.K. Rowling's darkest hour?

Here's how she describes that time in her life:
"An exceptionally short-lived marriage had imploded, and I was jobless, a lone parent, and as poor as it is possible to be in modern Britain, without being homeless . . . I was the biggest failure I knew. I was set free, because my greatest fear had been realized, and I was still alive, and I still had a daughter whom I adored, and I had an old typewriter and a big idea. And so rock bottom became the solid foundation on which I rebuilt my life."[4]

So, Rowling captured the imagination of a generation with a story.

The story of a boy named Harry—
an unusual boy, marked for a specific destiny from birth.

As he discovered his true identity and embraced his purpose, he grew in wisdom and strength.
His closest friends followed him everywhere, facing grave opposition, but they could not always understand what he understood.
They could not follow him into the very final battle against an evil enemy, where he entered into death itself . . . and defeated it.

Sounds familiar, doesn't it?
Regardless of what you think about Harry,
you have to agree.

Stories are powerful.
Especially when they reflect God's story.

Stories over time matter.
Especially when they come from parents and leaders who care.

So, do whatever you can to amplify the best stories around you.

READ **THEM.**
WATCH **THEM.**
TELL **THEM.**
CREATE **THEM.**
WRITE **THEM.**
ILLUSTRATE **THEM.**
FILM **THEM.**
LIVE **THEM.**
COLLECT **THEM.**

Stories can make history for a child.
Stories can transform his or her perspective.

They can make
life fuller,
faith deeper,
hope stronger.

STORIES OVER TIME
MOVE US TO IMAGINE
A WORLD BEYOND
OURSELVES.

PLAY *for* KEEPS

HABIT 4

AMPLIFY THE STORY

Select stories to inspire them

SO WHY DO YOU THINK WE WROTE A STORY ABOUT
A KID NAMED SIMON?

WE NEEDED A CREATIVE OUTLET
WE WANTED AN EXCUSE TO GO TO MEMPHIS
IT WAS DIVINELY INSPIRED

No.
It may just be because we have a high view of fiction.
It's okay if you don't.

Maybe for you, the thought of reading about made-up people
experiencing pretend realities seems trivial. You want the real world.
You want someone to "give it to you straight." That's fine. We wrote
this half of the book for you.

But we tend to think that with fiction we can . . .
say more through specific characters,
leave the necessary tensions unresolved,
break down barriers of communication,
and invite you into something that's more emotionally engaging.

So we amplified the story. We introduced you to Eric. Because we just
figured he's a guy you need to know.

Fiction isn't the only way to tell a story.
And some of the best stories aren't fiction.
But if you have a message to share, one of the best ways you can
communicate that message is with a story.

That's why you need stories if you want to influence someone's
perspective. As parents and leaders, maybe it's time for you to start
using the time you have to get serious about amplifying the story for
the kids who matter most in your lives.

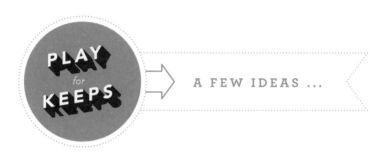

A FEW IDEAS ...

DISCOVER THE ARTS

Yes, that's what we mean. It's pretty simple. If you want to shape the perspectives of the kids and teenagers you care about, you will always be looking for new stories.

HERE'S THE GOOD NEWS:

STORIES ARE EVERYWHERE.

EXPERIENCING THEM CAN BE FUN.

So this week, discover the arts together.
Experience them.
Participate in them.
Talk about them together.

THAT MEANS. . .
WATCH A MOVIE.
READ A BOOK.
GO TO A PLAY.
SING A SONG.
VISIT A MUSEUM.
DRAW A PICTURE.
APPRECIATE HISTORY.
WRITE A POEM.
LISTEN TO A CONCERT.
PAINT A PAINTING.
ATTEND A BALLET.

Oh yeah, and one more thing—
When you go looking for all these stories, don't forget about *The Story*.
It's not that every story you experience with a kid or teenager has to
be biblical or even overtly Christian. They shouldn't be. But if you look
closely enough, you will discover moments when you can highlight
God's story of restoration and redemption.

Maybe that's why the psalmist says,

"I WILL OPEN MY MOUTH WITH A PARABLE;
I WILL UTTER HIDDEN THINGS, THINGS FROM OF OLD—
THINGS WE HAVE HEARD AND KNOWN,
THINGS OUR ANCESTORS HAVE TOLD US.
WE WILL NOT HIDE THEM FROM THEIR DESCENDANTS;
WE WILL TELL THE NEXT GENERATION
THE PRAISEWORTHY DEEDS OF THE LORD,
HIS POWER, AND THE WONDERS HE HAS DONE."[5]

Because every week, you have an opportunity to tell *the story* to the
next generation in a way that will captivate their imagination and

move them not only to fall in love with the story itself, but to fall in love with the God who created the story and who has invited them to be a part of it.

I'm not sure if hymnist Katherine Hankey spent much time around children and teenagers. But if she did, that would explain why she wrote these words:
"I love to tell the story,
'twill be my theme in glory,
to tell the old, old story of Jesus and His love."[6]

CAPTURE THE STORYLINE

In a world where everyone with a smartphone has access to a high-def camera 24/7, we have all become photojournalists. We're literally obsessed with telling our stories. That's why we . . .
post it on a blog,
share it on Instagram,
tag it on Facebook,
upload it to Shutterfly.

You really don't need to be told to take more pictures.

But capturing the storyline is about more than just taking pictures to share with your online community. When you capture the storyline for a kid or teenager, you look for ways to record and re-tell significant stories in their lives so you can give them the a relational history that fuels a healthy perspective about their identity.

So, **record it.**

There are many parents and leaders who record key moments in a
journal,
baby book,
shoe box,
three-ring binder,
or box of note cards.

Or maybe even with significant objects like . . .
a Thanksgiving turkey made of multi-colored handprints.
a plastic souvenir cup from your trip to Disney World.
a third-place ribbon from the fourth-grade spelling bee.
the playbill from Andersonville Middle School's production of *Wizard
of Oz.*
the movie stubs from all three times you went to see *Never Say Never.*

You don't have to make or keep everything on this list. Just do a few
things. Figure out what fits your style and accomplishes the goal.

You also capture the storyline when you **re-tell it.**

You do this every time you begin a conversation with . . .
"I remember when you . . . "
"That time when we all got together and . . ."
"You have always been so good at . . ."

This is one place where parents may have more opportunities than leaders—because they tend to be connected to the storyline over a longer period of time. And let's face it, if you are a leader who is *too* good at this, it could be a little creepy. But if you lead a group for any significant amount of time—from a few months to multiple years—you can find ways to record and re-tell the story of your group. You also have an opportunity to help parents record and re-tell the story for their kids.

If you're a parent, you should also look for ways to record and re-tell your own story and the story of your family history. You might write it in a journal, build a photo-album, or record a video. No two families are alike. Your family stories have a significant role to play in giving your child the relational history they need.

Remember, whether you are a parent or leader, you don't have to be the most creative, artistic, scrapbooking-Pinterest-expert to do this well. If you are, that's fantastic. But know that whatever seemingly small things you're already doing to capture the storyline will have a lasting impact on the perspectives of the kids and teenagers you love.

GET IN THE ACTION

Good stories don't just happen. You have to create them. As a leader or parent, you are an author. Okay, never mind, we only wish we had that kind of control. We know that God is ultimately the author of the story. But you do have influence with a few characters; so think for a minute about your influence the way an author might think.

If you are influencing a leading character . . .
What qualities do you want your character to develop?
What lessons does your character need to learn?
What experiences does your character need to have?

Or maybe you could think about it this way:
As they begin their epic journey, every good hero needs
surmountable obstacles
sidekicks
super powers

If you figure out how to give them super powers, let us know. That
would be impressive. We'll talk more about sidekicks in the next
chapter. What about surmountable obstacles? Every author knows if you
want a leading character to develop the virtues necessary to triumph,
you need to architect some character-building experiences along the
way. As an "author," or influencer, you have an opportunity to help kids
discover challenges, face obstacles, and participate in the action.

You may want to add something to their storyline like . . .
volunteering at a food bank.
taking an annual mission trip.
packing a shoebox.
raising money for a non-profit.

As you look for opportunities to build their stories and get them into
the action, remember two things:
THEY NEED TO EXPERIENCE FAILURE.
THEY NEED TO EXPERIENCE SUCCESS.

That may seem contradictory, but experts seem to agree on these two things. On the one hand, kids and teenagers need to be surrounded by adults who will resist the temptation to jump into situations to "solve it" for them. They need leaders and parents who will love them enough to let them navigate challenges early on while the stakes are lower, so they will be better equipped to face adulthood when the consequences may be more severe.

On the other hand, it's important to involve kids and teenagers in experiences where they can succeed.

My (Reggie) oldest daughter grew up playing basketball. In the ninth grade, her coach made an unusual decision. He decided that since the team was especially young, he would only have them play scrimmages instead of playing in the normal league. Many of the players' parents were upset.
He wasn't pushing them.
He wasn't stretching them.
He wasn't challenging their ability as a team.

But here's the reason he gave: he wanted the team to understand what it felt like to win. He knew that letting his team get overwhelmed by older, more seasoned players could potentially ingrain in them a sense of failure. It wasn't that he never wanted them to lose; he just wanted the team to experience enough wins in order to understand their potential and get in the habit of being successful.

WHAT'S THE POINT?

AS YOU LOOK FOR WAYS TO ENGAGE
KIDS AND TEENAGERS IN THE ACTION,
REMEMBER THE VALUE OF PLANNING
FOR THEIR SUCCESS. YOU WANT THEM
TO BE A LEADING CHARACTER WITH
THE KIND OF OPTIMISM THAT KEEPS
JUMPING BACK INTO THE ACTION,
AGAIN AND AGAIN.

Remember, as parents and leaders, when you amplify the story,
you are giving kids and teenagers a bigger story perspective.

You aren't just teaching them lessons about life, faith, and love.
You are connecting them to a story that's bigger than themselves.

That's what story does over time.
It gives a child or teenager the kind of perspective that says,
"God's story moves me to a sense of wonder.
I am amazed at how His story intersects with my story.
And I realize that I matter in the stories of others—that we are living out
our story together."

It really is a story of love.

So what you do to amplify the story this week matters.
Connect kids and teenagers with cultural, relational, and spiritual stories.
Help them imagine a world beyond themselves.

From the Losing Your Marbles story

BETWEEN THE LINES

THINK ABOUT

ERIC

Eric is an authentic and independent high school senior—not to mention a ridiculously talented musician. It's no wonder Simon likes to hang around him. He's gutsy enough to be honest with himself and chase his own ambitions rather than simply satisfying the expectations of others.

Sure, he would probably swear more.
We didn't want to offend anyone, so we cleaned him up a bit.

But even though Eric is a generally likeable guy, he is still a self-centered kid whose primary focus is his own success. He has imagined a narrowly-focused story for himself—one centered on personal ambition and fame.

Until . . .

A kid named Simon invites him to church.
A small group leader named Ken prompts him to consider his story.

Not knowing what to expect, Eric shows up for Simon and his group of

From the Losing Your Marbles story

BETWEEN THE LINES

zombies. He is moved by the story he sees them living out together—especially as he tunes in to Simon's story. He discovers there is more to Simon than he's ever taken time to discover. And even though there is no apparent personal benefit, Eric begins to get more involved in Simon's world.

With Ken's inspiration, Eric realizes he has a role to play in the stories of others just as they have a role to play in his. Eric chooses to get in the action and help Simon in his elaborate plan to save Max. In the process, Eric finds meaning and purpose when his story becomes more connected to the stories of others. He is moved to imagine a world beyond himself.

KNUCKLE DOWN:

Write down some of the stories that have redefined the way you see yourself and others—fictional or real. What are some new ways you can engage kids in stories that will move them beyond themselves?

**WHAT YOU DO THIS WEEK TO EXPERIENCE
STORIES WITH A KID OR TEENAGER MATTERS.**

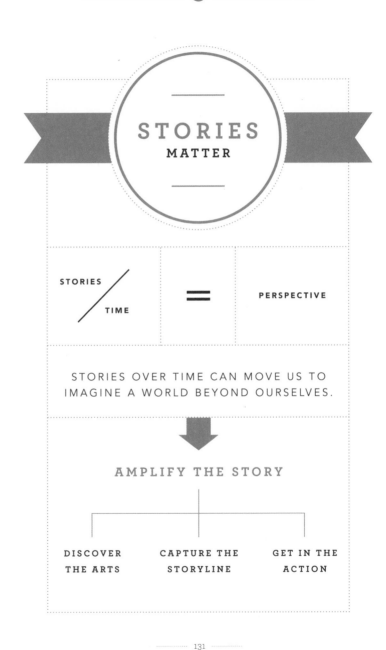

STORIES
MATTER

$$\frac{STORIES}{TIME} = PERSPECTIVE$$

STORIES OVER TIME CAN MOVE US TO
IMAGINE A WORLD BEYOND OURSELVES.

AMPLIFY THE STORY

| DISCOVER THE ARTS | CAPTURE THE STORYLINE | GET IN THE ACTION |

TRIBES

over

TIME

SHOW US HOW
WE BELONG

TRIBES

Matter

TRIBES
Matter

Everyone's familiar with the way it feels.
It can happen when you . . .
walk into a room of strangers.
look for a seat in the school cafeteria.
wear your Tar Heels jersey to Cameron Stadium.

It's just the way you feel when you are on the outside looking in.
Something tells you this is not your
family,
friends,
or tribe,
and you obviously don't belong.

It's easy to feel
Awkward
Uncomfortable
Alone

Those feelings don't have a long-term effect when they happen
occasionally.
We're resilient.
We're optimistic.
We believe we will find our seat at the table.
So we keep moving until we land somewhere.

Our drive to belong is the reason . . .
people take showers.
synchronized swimming has fans.
men stopped wearing leisure suits in the seventies.
Tom Hanks apologized to a soccer ball named Wilson.

WE ARE ALL
TRYING TO FIT IN
SOMEWHERE.

BUT NOT BELONGING CAN BE DEVASTATING IF . . .
the loneliness is consistent.
the isolation is frequent.
the rejection is recurrent.

If you grow up without a tribe, it can complicate things—and the complications of not belonging over time can seriously impair the future of a child.

According to Stanford Professor Gregory Walton, "Isolation, loneliness and low social status can harm a person's subjective sense of well-being, as well as his or her intellectual achievement, immune function and health."[1]

BASICALLY,

PEOPLE NEED PEOPLE.

EVERYBODY NEEDS A CIRCLE,

AND EVERY KID NEEDS A TRIBE.

What exactly is a tribe?
It's simply a group of people connected by something in common.
Ancestry
Ideas
Experiences
Politics
Theology
Sports

WE DEFINE OURSELVES BY TRIBES.

I AM A . . .

Musician	*Foodie*	*Republican*
Baptist	*Conservative*	*Reader*
Feminist	*Mom*	*Artist*
Braves fan	*Student*	*Blogger*
Photojournalist	*Biker*	***Pirate***

If you meet someone from that last group, you will instantly know who they are. They will probably be wearing an eye patch, have a scruffy beard, bad breath, and if you make them mad you will hear them say, "Aaarrr." That probably goes for the next-to-last group, too.

Tribes give us opportunities to connect with a variety of people.
It's how humans find other humans.

Tribes give you a wide range of relational choices.
They offer circles for you to move in and out of as you discover who you are and where you belong.

English novelist Jane Howard said it this way, "Call it a clan, call it a network, call it a tribe, call it a family: Whatever you call it, whoever you are, you need one."[2]

WE ALL NEED A TRIBE—WHETHER IT'S LARGE OR SMALL.

So, you might be thinking,
"Is a small group a tribe?"—not really.
"Is my family a tribe?"—kind of.

Small groups and families both help us understand the power of what happens in a tribe. They both give us a significant place to belong.

AS A LEADER OR PARENT, YOU PLAY A CRITICAL ROLE IN
CONNECTING KIDS TO TWO PRIMARY TRIBES.

THE CHURCH   THE FAMILY

Just like love, words, and stories were God's idea, so were tribes.

Think back again to creation.
God didn't want Adam to be alone—so Eve came along.
Then other people started showing up.
(It's really not complicated to figure out how that happened.)

People were always part of God's plan.
Maybe that's why tribes matter so much.
They exist to remind us that
we belong to God and
we belong together.

When God wanted to redeem His creation,
He started with a tribe—okay, twelve tribes.
He created a nation and set them apart.
They had their own faith, customs, and traditions.

Then, through that nation, God sent His Son.
And something interesting began to happen.
Ecclesias, small tribes, began to appear all around the Mediterranean.
They ate together.
They prayed together.
They had their own values and distinctives.

Then Paul wrote letters to connect these smaller tribes with each other.
He helped them understand what they had in common.
He helped them navigate similar struggles.
He wrote down customs, beliefs, theology, and instruction to help define
the larger tribe to which they all belonged. It was a group of people
connected by a common trust in the death and resurrection of Jesus.

The idea began to spread.
The tribe grew.

IT'S AS IF GOD DESIGNED US SO WE
WOULD NATURALLY CONNECT IN **TRIBES**.
THEN HE USED **TRIBES** OVER TIME
TO REVEAL HIMSELF TO US, AND TO
CONTINUE TO SPREAD HIS MESSAGE
OF LOVE.

Tribes are just another one of God's genius ideas. So genius in fact, that leaders today are considered genius for using tribes to spread their ideas.

Consider Seth Godin's explanation of how tribes work, "It's tribes—not money, not factories—that can change our world . . . not because we force people to do something against their will, but because they want to connect." Godin explains how leveraging our human longing for connection is the best vehicle for the spread of an idea. According to Godin, when you assemble tribes that assemble tribes, they spread the idea so that it becomes a movement. [3]

Isn't it interesting that marketing experts are just discovering the same technique God has used to spread His message through generations since the beginning of time?

But the original purpose of tribes was not marketing. It was missional: to connect people to the message of a loving God who pursued a relationship with them over time.

TRIBES HAVE MATTERED FOR A LONG TIME.

THEY MATTER BECAUSE THEY ARE ONE OF GOD'S
PRIMARY WAYS TO COMMUNICATE HIS LOVE FOR US.

The Pharisees, as religious leaders, failed to understand that mission. They understood the value of keeping the practices and traditions of the tribe of faith. But they failed to understand the value of a tribe in making people feel welcomed, accepted, and loved by God. Instead, they had a reputation for judging and rejecting people who didn't perform by their standards.

SO JESUS CONFRONTED THEM ONE DAY.
HE TOLD A STORY ABOUT A FAMILY WITH TWO SONS:

The youngest left home prematurely. He took his father's inheritance and went to the "far country." It was his big chance. He hoped to build his own fortune, find new friends, and leave his mark on the world. Unfortunately, due to a series of wrong decisions—and the fact he had never taken any of Dave Ramsey's courses—he lost everything.

Basically, he ended up working at a BBQ place in south Georgia. Even worse, he had to live out back with the pigs. I'm sure you've heard the story about how he finally said one day, "I wanna go home." (I can almost hear Michael Bublé singing.)

I can imagine the prodigal son walking across the last field toward the big white house where he grew up. (At least in my mind, it's a big white house.)

His loving father runs to meet him and gives him a hug, despite what had to be an awful odor.

Why?
Because according to his dad,
"My son was lost, now he is found."

Translated:
My son lost his way,
now he's back where he belongs.

He was a smart dad who knew tribes matter.

So he did two things:
He gave his son a ring to remind him he still belonged in the family.
He threw his son a party to assure him that he still had a community where he belonged.

He wanted to send a clear message,
"There's still a seat for you at our table.
This is a place where . . .
You are known.
You are welcome.
You are forgiven.
YOU BELONG."

That's something only tribes can do.
And the tribes most strategically positioned to do that are
The family.
The church.

Kids and teenagers desperately need people who . . .
know them,
welcome them,
and forgive them
over time so they will know they belong.

Remember education reformer Geoffrey Canada? He says kids need to grow up with a certain level of failure so they can understand it's possible to move beyond their mistakes. But they also need to know they can be forgiven, both by their parents and by other adults as well. Canada says this is where church leaders make a difference. This is actually what a tribe of faith should be best at doing—reminding kids they are forgiven by the people who know them best.[4]

We all want to be known by someone. We want to know: regardless of whatever failure we have in our life, we still have a place to belong and people who believe in us.

THIS IDEA OF BELONGING IS
ACTUALLY WHAT MAKES OUR FAITH AS
CHRISTIANS DISTINCTIVE.

OUR SENSE OF BELONGING IS ROOTED
IN THE CONCEPT OF GRACE.

GRACE MEANS . . .

YOU DON'T BELONG BECAUSE YOU DESERVE TO BELONG.
YOU BELONG BECAUSE GOD HAS ACCEPTED AND
FORGIVEN YOU.
YOU ARE KNOWN BY GOD IN A WAY YOU ARE NOT KNOWN
BY ANYONE, (EVERY THOUGHT, EVERY DESIRE, EVERY ACTION),
AND YET HE HAS WELCOMED YOU INTO HIS TRIBE FOREVER.

THAT'S
BELONGING.

It's important to introduce children and teenagers to the grace of God
when they are young. It may be the greatest thing you can do for their
sense of belonging.

At some point, most of us have experienced what happens when
someone doesn't feel like they belong.

When Debbie and I (Reggie) met Alyssa,
she convinced us she needed a heart transplant—
It wasn't a scam for money, but it was a scam for attention.

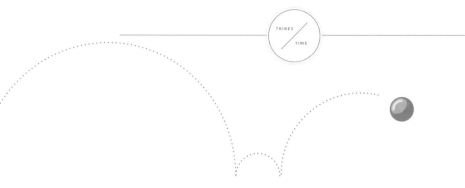

She had played this game most of her young life.
To impress someone.
To belong somewhere.

Her history was filled with the fictions she told in an attempt to earn
acceptance. But eventually . . .
she was caught,
her pretenses were exposed,
everyone knew the truth,
and she felt alone again.

Then, at twenty-two she failed at the first attempt to take her life.

Debbie and I waited at Elmhurst hospital for three days before she
would agree to see us. When she did see us, she was angry.

Her first words were,
"I don't want you here. Why did you come?
I really don't want to talk about anything."

She was slow to warm up, but she did. Maybe it was the chocolate we
brought or the fact that she was tired of the crowd in the psych ward.

After a few visits she asked this question:
"Why would you come back after knowing what I did?"

For me, it was simple: we knew her.
There was obviously a part we didn't know.
But there was also a part of her we did know.

Beneath the façade and pretense there was a
Smart
Savvy
Creative
Ambitious
Daring
Lively
Sarcastic
girl who was the age of our own daughters.

I think that's what we saw.
She was someone's daughter who had been trapped in her life by a string of bad choices while she tried to figure out where and how to belong.

So I said, "Alyssa, the reason we came back is *because* we know what you did. Sometimes you just need someone in your life who knows what you did and who shows up anyway. I need that. I need to be loved by the people who have history with me. Otherwise, how can I really know I'm loved?"

Alyssa was not that different than you or me. She just needed tribes over time where she could be known and forgiven in spite of what she had done.

JUST REMEMBER:

YOU CAN'T FEEL FORGIVEN BY PEOPLE WHO
DON'T REALLY KNOW YOU.

THAT'S WHY KIDS NEED TRIBES OVER TIME.

KIDS NEED	**KIDS NEED**	**KIDS NEED**
TO BE KNOWN	**TO BE KNOWN**	**TO BE KNOWN**
before they can	before they can	before they can
feel welcome.	feel forgiven.	feel like they belong.

So when they show up
broken,
lonely,
and wounded,
make sure they know they have
a seat at your table.

Be the kind of parent or leader who will . . .
give them a ring.
throw them a party.

> Because there are two things that will make your home and church
> attractive to kids and teenagers:
> FORGIVENESS
> JOY
> (We'll talk more about Joy in the next chapter.)

**IF YOU WANT TO CREATE A PLACE WHERE KIDS WANT TO BE,
OR MORE IMPORTANTLY WHERE THEY WILL RUN BACK TO WHEN
LIFE HAS BROKEN THEM,**

GIVE THEM
A TRIBE
OVER TIME.

HABIT 5

GO IN CIRCLES

*Help them
experience community*

It's just another way of saying,
"Do life in the context of relationships."
Kids need to be encouraged early in life to connect in tribes and groups.

If you've ever . . .
been on a retreat,
volunteered at a VBS,
or chaperoned a field trip,
you understand the value of going in circles.

You tell kids all the time, "Go in groups."
There's safety in numbers. No one gets lost, and you are more likely to
know about it if someone gets hurt.

What is true physically is also true emotionally.
There is a long-term psychological benefit to "going in a group."

WHEN YOU GO IN A GROUP, YOU
UNDERSTAND HOW YOU BELONG.
YOU FEEL CONNECTED TO A TRIBE
BECAUSE YOU HAVE SOMETHING
IN COMMON.

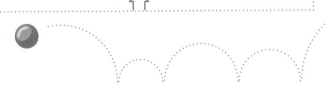

Tribes are like circles—and everyone goes in different kinds of circles.

You probably have an *INNER* CIRCLE made up of your closest friends
and family.
Then you have some *SOCIAL* CIRCLES based on your interests,
hobbies, or profession.
You have a *SPIRITUAL* CIRCLE made up of the people with whom
you worship.
And we all belong to a *GLOBAL* CIRCLE of people who are connected
simply because we have all been made in the image of God.

The point is we all go in circles.
And the circles we go in over time will give us a place where we can be
Known
Welcomed
Forgiven

So, as leaders and parents,
consider how you help a kid go in circles.

In other words, think about how they . . .
eat in circles.
travel in circles.
play in circles.
work in circles.
learn in circles.

IF KIDS NEED TO CONNECT IN TRIBES OVER TIME IN ORDER
TO UNDERSTAND HOW THEY BELONG, WE AS PARENTS AND
LEADERS NEED TO BE INTENTIONAL ABOUT HOW WE CREATE
CIRCLES THAT WILL MAKE THEM FEEL LIKE THEY ARE A PART
OF A TRIBE.

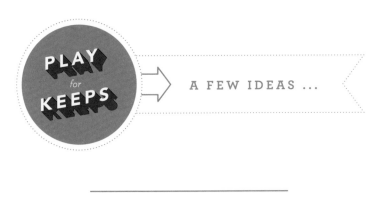

A FEW IDEAS ...

KEEP A TRADITION

Nothing helps define a tribe like traditions.

They are shared unique practices, and only insiders fully understand their significance to the group. If you want to create a feeling of solidarity for your tribe, you should have a few traditions.

You may keep some seasonal traditions.
As a leader, maybe you . . .
celebrate an end-of-the-school-year party.
have an annual tithe plate discus competition.
take a seniors-only retreat after graduation Sunday.

As a parent, maybe you . . .
have a special birthday hat.
take a fall camping trip.
cut down your own Christmas tree.
host a "summer Olympics" for the neighborhood in your backyard.

You probably have some weekly traditions.
As a leader, maybe you . . .
refer to your group by a special name.
share highs and lows from the week.
hold hands when you pray.

As a parent, maybe you . . .
spend Saturday morning in bed.
have a Friday movie night.
eat breakfast for dinner every Wednesday.
FaceTime with grandparents on the weekends.

It's also important to have a few verbal traditions.
What? You thought we already talked about words? Okay, we did. It's
just that some words really function more like traditions than anything
else. They are like inside jokes. When you know them, you know you
are a part of a tribe.

If you hang out with a tribe long enough, you will develop some
common language. In his book, *Talk the Talk*, Luc Reid documents "the
slang of 65 American subcultures." In essence, he looks for way to
articulate the verbal traditions of a group. In his introduction, he says,
"Subcultural slang is more than a specialized vocabulary. Adopting
slang is a way to invite people in or to keep casual onlookers out;
. . . of confirming or denying relationships; of marking your particular
territory in . . . [a tribe]."[5]

 SO, WHAT IS YOUR COMMON LANGUAGE? WHAT ARE
THE PHRASES YOU USE ON A REGULAR BASIS THAT
MAKE YOUR GROUP OR YOUR FAMILY UNIQUE?

As believers, we are all part of a tribe that keeps spiritual traditions.
These are the traditions that extend beyond our church, beyond our
country, and beyond our generation in order to connect us to a tribe of
believers that has existed since the first century.

> WE PARTICIPATE IN
> BAPTISM
> COMMUNION
> WORSHIP
> AS PART OF A SPIRITUAL HERITAGE.

Depending on your denomination, you may apply a variety of meanings
to these traditions, but regardless of how much water you use or how
much alcohol is or isn't in the cup, these traditions connect you to a
tribe of faith.

EAT A MEAL

This "idea" is probably the most important one in the book.
We actually thought about calling the book, *Food Matters.*
That's because without food, nothing else really matters, right?

If someone is in your tribe, you will probably eat together at some point.

No matter who you are, food plays a significant role in your life. After
all, we eat every day. So if you want to do something *over time* that will
give a kid a sense of belonging, it only makes sense that you will eat
with them.

Not only is eating one of the most predictable and unchanging routines in our life, it also plays a role in our most significant moments.

I BET YOU CAN TELL ME WHAT . . .

Mother's Day	*New Year's Day*	*Birthdays*
July Fourth	*Thanksgiving*	*Christmas*
Weddings	*Valentine's Day*	*Easter*

. . . TASTE LIKE.

THE TASTES AND SMELLS OF FOOD
MAKE AN IMPRINT ON OUR MEMORIES.
IF YOU WANT SOMEONE TO KNOW THEY
BELONG IN YOUR TRIBE, SIT WITH
THEM AND SHARE A MEAL.

If you're a leader, you probably won't be eating daily meals with the kids and teenagers you serve. And if you're honest, sharing food weekly requires a lot more planning, introduces some tricky complications, and ends up making a really big mess. But don't let it stop you from experiencing the joy of eating together.

KIDS LISTEN BETTER WHEN THEY'RE NOT HUNGRY.

That's why some student ministries schedule their programming in the evening so leaders and teenagers have a weekly opportunity to share a meal together.

It's also why one of the smartest high school small group leaders I know brings a "snack bucket" to group every week, and that bucket has become one of the hallmarks of their tribe.

If you're a parent, you've probably already heard all the statistics about family mealtime. For the past decade, research has inundated us with the message that families who eat (especially dinner) together are happier, healthier, have kids who do better in school, and have teenagers who engage in fewer risky behaviors. Some recent studies now argue that the family meal is more a characteristic of healthy families than the root cause of family health.

Either way, "There is something about a shared meal . . . that anchors a family."[6] Meals provide families with a routine opportunity to connect relationally and share an experience together. Professor William Doherty, author of The Intentional Family: Simple Rituals to Strengthen Family Ties, reminds us, "Meals are where a family builds its identity and culture. Legends are passed down, jokes rendered, eventually the wider world examined through the lens of a family's values."[7] It's not the food that magically makes a kid belong. But since we all have to eat anyway, you have an opportunity to leverage eating as a time when you can routinely connect with each other over time.

SO EAT TOGETHER. BUT REMEMBER:

It doesn't have to be dinner.
It doesn't have to be every day.
It doesn't have to be gourmet.
It doesn't have to be at home.
IT JUST HAS TO BE TOGETHER.

FIND THEM A SEAT

As the leader of a tribe, you have a unique role: think like a host. If you are a host, you know one of your key responsibilities is to make sure everyone has a seat. You don't want anyone left standing. You want them to know they have a place reserved just for them.

Remember Forrest Gump? As a kindergartner, he makes the long walk down the aisle of the school bus where kid after kid communicates the same message: "Seat's taken!" Then he hears "the sweetest voice in the wide world," Jenny's voice:

"You can sit here if you like."

THERE WILL ALWAYS BE KIDS WHO DON'T HAVE A SEAT. YOUR ROLE IS TO IDENTIFY THOSE KIDS AND FIND THEM A SEAT IN A CIRCLE—TO GIVE THEM A CHANCE TO BELONG.

IF YOU'RE A LEADER, THAT'S WHY YOU SHOW UP WEEK AFTER WEEK TO DO WHAT YOU DO—TO GIVE KIDS A SEAT. BUT DON'T LIMIT YOUR PERSPECTIVE TO ONLY THOSE WHO ARE ALREADY INSIDE YOUR CIRCLES.

When I (Reggie) was a student pastor, I charged a group of students with the responsibility of hosting our environments. That meant they were constantly identifying anyone who was standing alone and connecting that person with a group. The task was simple: Make sure no one stays alone. Get them a seat in the circle. Don't let this next statement minimize the need for adult leaders, but for this specific task, it was more effective for teenagers to act as the hosts of our environment. High school students will respond more when they feel included by their peers.

If you're a parent, you are constantly looking for circles where you can give your kid a seat. You give them a seat in your own family circle. But you also give them a seat in spiritual circles when you make it a priority to take them to a church with consistent leaders. And you give them a seat in social circles when you take them to dance, soccer, drama, or anime club.

Helping kids connect in circles isn't a science. You can't manufacture chemistry, and you can't force connection. But you can look for kids and adults who share a common interest with your child and make an introduction.

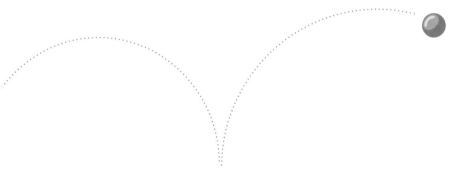

Then remember, they may need a little guidance.
It may not be as spiritual as teaching them Psalm 23, as intellectual as
helping them learn to read, or as physically rigorous as coaching them
to hit a baseball, but kids also need parents and leaders who can help
them learn to . . .
make a new friend,
resolve a conflict,
deal with rejection,
and include others,
if you want them to belong in tribes over time.

What you do to connect kids and teenagers in tribes this week matters.
Because every child needs a place to belong and people who believe
in them over time.

IT'S HOW THEY
WILL KNOW THEY ARE
WELCOME. IT'S HOW THEY
WILL FEEL FORGIVEN.
IT MAY BE THE BEST WAY
FOR THEM TO UNDERSTAND
THE CONCEPT
OF GRACE.

From the Losing Your Marbles story

BETWEEN THE LINES

THINK ABOUT

MAX

You might not typically consider finding a seat at the lunch table a traumatic experience. But for Max, it's terrifying. And it happens every day.

Uprooted from his childhood friends, Max is alone in a new school. Everything is different in Memphis: The style is different; the accepted music is different; the slang is different; the jokes are different. Sure, he's been around for almost a year now. But he can still walk from one end of the lunchroom to the other not knowing if someone will have thought to save him a seat. At twelve, every kid can feel out of place, but Max feels like even more of an outsider.

He's alone in a crowd,
painfully self-aware,
and looking to find a group.

Max's need for a tribe makes him vulnerable. He will do whatever it takes to find a circle—even if it means jeopardizing the school and potentially hurting others in the process. He is positioned to make a

From the Losing Your Marbles story

BETWEEN THE LINES

series of unwise choices, not because he is a bad kid, but because he isn't connected.

With insight uncanny for a twelve-year-old, Simon understands what Max really needs is for someone to let him in. He needs a tribe.

He needs a group of people who . . .
know his name,
care if he shows up,
get his jokes,
and accept him.

He needs to belong somewhere so he can feel like he matters.

Max is caught off-guard by a group of eccentric zombies—not just because they thwart his kidnapping, but because they cheer him on and accept him without questions. It's this spark of connection that gives Max the courage to face his father honestly. This may not be the answer to all of Max's issues, but it certainly is a hopeful beginning.

KNUCKLE DOWN:

What traditions and habits have you adopted that you think make your kids feel most connected? Are there any traditions you should change or start that will make them feel more connected?

**WHAT YOU DO THIS WEEK TO CONNECT KIDS
AND TEENAGERS IN A TRIBE MATTERS.**

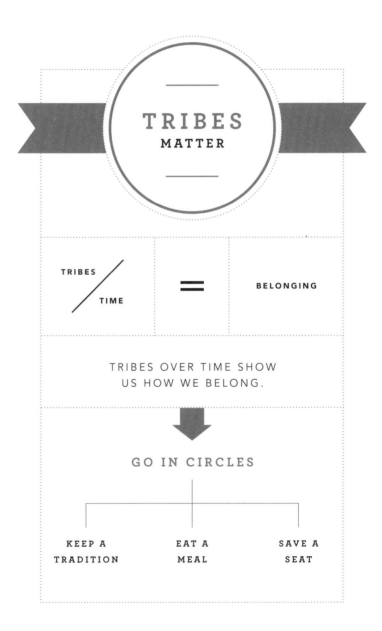

TRIBES
MATTER

TRIBES / TIME = BELONGING

TRIBES OVER TIME SHOW
US HOW WE BELONG.

GO IN CIRCLES

| KEEP A TRADITION | EAT A MEAL | SAVE A SEAT |

FUN

——— *over* ———

TIME

MAKES A FRIENDSHIP
GO DEEPER

FUN

Matters

Matters

That's why we want to remind you again to "*play* for keeps."
And we do mean that literally.

In other words,
it's important that you actually play.

And when we say play,
we mean play in the context of

PLAY BALL

PLAY GAMES

PLAYROOM

PLAY MAKE-BELIEVE

PLAY HIDE-AND-SEEK

PLAYSTATION

PLAY CARDS

PLAYACT

PLAYGROUND

PLAY-DOH

FUN / TIME

STATED SIMPLY:
ONE OF THE MOST
EFFECTIVE WAYS TO
STAY CONNECTED
TO YOUR KIDS IS TO
HAVE FUN
WITH THEM.

What do we mean by fun?
Pretty much anything that
entertains them,
makes them laugh,
and helps them enjoy life.

Really?
Anything?
No.

You should probably leave out things like . . .
skating in traffic.
wrestling with alligators.
sticking forks in electrical outlets.
jumping ramps with baby strollers.
launching bottle rockets from body parts.

You're the adult, so we expect you to screen some things with a little
common sense.

There are definitely some fun things that kids shouldn't do because
they're . . .
not safe,
not age-appropriate,
or they break a major commandment.

But be careful your *don't* list,
doesn't overshadow your *do* list,
or you could lose your kids.

If you want to play for keeps, try to give kids a bigger list of *do's*
than *dont's*.
Act like fun really matters—because it does to a kid.

KIDS WERE CREATED

WITH A "**PLAY**" DRIVE.

As were . . .
dolphins,
squirrels,
sparrows,
monkeys,
cats,
and unicorns.
(Okay, not that one, I'm just making sure you're still reading.)

Evidently fun matters so much to God, He decided to illustrate it everywhere in nature to remind us we need to play. If you don't believe me, you should just get a dog and count how many times you get nudged to throw a ball.

You were made to have fun.

But if you're like the average adult,
one day you grew out of it.

It's possible . . .
"You've lost that 'playing' feeling.
Now it's gone, gone, gone.
Whoa whoa oh."

Okay, maybe that's cheesy.
But we're just trying to stimulate you to have more fun.

Seriously?!
Yeah, seriously.

That's actually part of the problem.
Too many people, especially Christians, take themselves too seriously.
Just read their responses to blogs and YouTube postings.

No wonder we can't make fun the kind of priority
it should really be in the home and church.

If that last statement makes you a little uncomfortable, then maybe you need to be honest with yourself about why it bothers you. Be careful you don't "but" it away with phrases like . . .

"But it's not our job to entertain kids."
"But kids need to learn to be reverent."
"But life is not all fun and games."
"But how can kids learn if they're having so much fun?"
(Our staff has already heard all of these arguments.)

It may be time to admit you have a **serious problem**.
Translated: You have a **problem with being too serious**. And the only way to remedy your serious problem is to get uncomfortable long enough to get comfortable with the idea of having fun again.

YOU NEED A FUN ADJUSTMENT.

You may need to . . .
LAUGH A LITTLE MORE.
DANCE A LITTLE LONGER.
PLAY A LITTLE HARDER.

That is—
if you want kids and teenagers to *want* to show up and be around more.
if you want to build a deeper relationship with them.

Let's face it.
Most of us are more worried about kids
sinning than we are about them playing.

Here's a thought I will let you argue about with someone else.
It could be a healthy debate.

> MAYBE IT'S MORE OF A SIN NOT TO HAVE FUN THAN IT IS
> TO DO SOME FUN THINGS THAT ARE CONSIDERED SIN BY
> SOME PEOPLE.

And no.
I'm not talking about sex.

The point is we all realize this: *Sin can be fun.*
Somewhere along the way, we get confused and start thinking, *It's a sin to have fun.*
But maybe the truth is *It's a sin **not** to have fun.*

What if it's time to stop taking ourselves so seriously, and start getting serious about having fun?

God certainly seems to take fun seriously—so seriously that most of the time when He wants us to focus on our relationship with Him, He tells us to . . .
sing,
dance,
celebrate,
eat
drink *(lemonade)*,
and be joyful.

EVIDENTLY, HE WANTS US TO THINK OF
OUR RELATIONSHIP WITH HIM KIND OF
LIKE A PARTY.

AND EVERYBODY LIKES A GOOD PARTY—
ESPECIALLY KIDS.

He also seems to want us to party frequently.
Just remember all those feast days and holidays in the Old Testament.

No, fun doesn't trivialize our mission.
And yes, we are called to
self-discipline,
suffering,
and sacrifice.

Just make sure you don't leave out the joy.
We are also called to
celebrate,
fellowship,
live fully,
and enjoy.

FUN / TIME

It's more than just okay to have fun. It's actually a command—or at least a strong suggestion. The word **fun** may not be in the Bible, but all its relatives are there.

"May the righteous be **glad** . . ."
"Rejoice in the Lord always . . ."
"and a time to **dance** . . ."
"Celebrate a festival to the Lord . . ."
"A **cheerful** heart is good medicine . . ."
"Worship the Lord with **gladness** . . ."
"The fruit of the Spirit is . . . **joy** . . ."
"They . . . ate together with **glad** and sincere hearts."
"However many years anyone may live, let them **enjoy** them all."[1]

Basically, we were created and told by God to enjoy
ourselves,
each other,
and everything else God made.

It's not unlike the way God enjoyed creation.
He actually modeled the idea on the seventh day when He stopped and "rested." If you think that means He was so worn out from six hard days of creating that He took a nap, you probably need to revisit the creation story.

He merely paused to enjoy what He had made.
That's what we're invited to do as well.
Every day.
Every week.

Sometimes we just need to stop working our busy routine long enough to enjoy Him and what He has made.

Sunday should be the most fun day of our week.
If it's not, then maybe we should rethink what we are doing.

Just because Sunday is supposed to be holy or sacred doesn't mean it shouldn't be fun.
If you think holy and fun are completely exclusive terms, then you should also re-examine your theology. You are missing a fundamental principle about fun.

WE WERE MADE
TO ENJOY AND
TO BE ENJOYED.

Christians should be the first ones to value fun. But a lot of Christians act like fun is something we should add to our church program to evangelize non-Christians. Then we go to work trying to make them feel guilty about having so much fun.

In reality, fun should never be something we tack on. It should be woven into our everyday lifestyles.

Christians should be the most
Joyful
Positive
Happy
Playful
Fun people
on the planet.

Instead, too many get a rap for being
negative,
pessimistic,
obnoxious,
judgmental,
and boring.

At the risk of oversimplifying—
If we played, laughed, danced, and smiled a little more, at church
and at home, kids and teenagers might grow up with a healthier
perspective on their family and Christian community.

Research reinforces the idea that fun matters. Some experts even
suggest people have a "play history" that holds the key to their
emotional and relational health. One such expert, Stuart Brown, warns
about the dangers of "play deprivation," especially when kids are
young. As a result of 30 years of research, he has concluded that it's
crucial for kids and adults to keep playing. According to Brown, "The
opposite of play is not work, it's depression." He goes on to claim
when you use neuroimaging techniques, "Nothing lights up the brain
like play."[2]

That's just another reason to play.
It adds a little energy to your relationship.

When you play with children and teenagers on their terms, you enter into their worlds. According to Lawrence J. Cohen, Ph.D., a psychologist and play therapist, "Play is where children show us the inner feelings and experiences that they can't or won't talk about. We need to hear what they have to say, and they need to share it. That's why we have to join children where they live, on their terms."[3] In other words, as parents and leaders, play actually opens the door so you can go deeper in your relationships with kids and teenagers.

SO START HAVING MORE FUN.

AND REMEMBER IT'S OKAY TO HAVE

FUN—JUST FOR FUN.

YOU WERE MADE TO HAVE FUN.

YOU WERE MADE TO HAVE FUN

TOGETHER.

Fun isn't a waste of time.
Fun over time can make your relationships go deeper.

FUN OVER TIME

> CONVINCES KIDS YOU ACTUALLY LIKE THEM.

I'm sure your kids know you love them.
But do they feel like you love them?
Before they can feel loved, they may need a little evidence that you like them. And they may never be confident that you like them, until you start having fun with them.

Sure, there are a lot of different ways to prove love.
We already said you should. . .
show up.
know them.
never run away.

But we just need to add one more to the list:
Have fun.

FUN OVER TIME

> RECONNECTS WHAT HAS BEEN DISCONNECTED.

Therapists have long known a secret that parents and leaders should learn:
Playing with kids breaks down walls.
It can repair damage in the relationship.

Playfulness is actually one effective way to deal with "tantrums, anxiety, sibling rivalry and even rebellious teen behavior."[4]

When something has come between you relationally, fun can be the bridge that rebuilds trust with each other.

FUN OVER TIME

FOSTERS RESILIENCE.

I know we already said it, but life is hard. If you want kids to grow up and push through heartbreak, tragedy, and disappointment, then they need a collection of fun memories to assure them . . .
that life goes on,
that the joys of living, loving, and laughing together far outweigh the pain that will also inevitably show up.

Having fun together helps us keep fighting for a relationship even when it's difficult.
Fun moves us to. . .
keep growing
keep caring
keep loving
—regardless.

FUN OVER TIME

AUTHENTICATES FORGIVENESS.

Fun may actually be one of the best ways to prove forgiveness
to someone.

Think about it:
How easy is it to have fun with someone if you are still offended by
what he or she did?

Remember, it's hard to fake forgiveness with kids.
They know better.
They are smart.
They will test you.
And they may not believe you've really forgiven them until you take the
initiative to have fun with them again.

Maybe that's why the Book of Romans says,
"Show mercy, cheerfully."[5]
How else can you prove it?

SOMETIMES WE CAN LEARN A LOT FROM KIDS.
THEY SEEM TO KNOW HOW TO MAKE FUN A PRIORITY, AND
THEY CAN ALSO BE QUICK TO FORGIVE AND MOVE ON. THEY
KNOW INTUITIVELY THAT FUN IS MORE IMPORTANT THAN
HOLDING GRUDGES.

FUN / TIME

HARRIET LERNER, PH.D., ILLUSTRATES THIS IN A STORY OF TWO
LITTLE KIDS PLAYING TOGETHER IN A SANDBOX.

"Suddenly a huge fight breaks out and one of the kids runs away
screaming, 'I hate you! I hate you!' In no time at all they're back in
the sandbox playing together happily again.

"Two adults observe the interaction from a nearby bench. 'Did you
see that?' one asks. 'How do children do that? They were enemies
five minutes ago.'

"'It's simple' the other replies. 'They choose happiness over
righteousness.'"[6]

As adult leaders and parents, we
need to take our cue from kids and
start acting like fun matters.

In the movie *Hook*, Robin Williams plays Peter Pan—not the adventurous, daring, vivacious, playful Peter. He portrays Peter Pan as an adult who is pre-occupied with adult issues.

In this scenario, Peter Pan is a dad with kids, but he's forgotten how to *be* a kid.

In one of the earlier scenes in the movie, Peter snaps at his children for interrupting a business call. His wife, while throwing his phone out the window, says,

"Your children love you, they want to play with you. How long do you think that lasts? Soon Jack may not even want you to come to his games. We have a few special years with our children, when they're the ones that want us around. After that you're going to be running after them for a bit of attention. It's so fast Peter. It's a few years, and it's over. And you are not being careful. And you are missing it."[7]

> THE POINT
> OF THE MOVIE TO
> EVERY ADULT IS SIMPLE:
> IF IT CAN HAPPEN TO
> PETER PAN, IT CAN
> HAPPEN TO ANY
> OF US.

Peter has simply grown up and forgotten how to play.
As a dad, he is missing out on the most critical years of his own
children's lives.

WHAT'S THE SOLUTION?
Peter has to . . .

rediscover his potential to play.

re-learn how to have fun with his kids.

reclaim his relationships through
an adventure.

start living like fun matters again.

HABIT 6

MAKE IT FUN

*Play and laugh
together more often*

I (Reggie) have a confession to make as a dad.
If I could go back in time, I would play more with my kids when they
were kids. It's not that we didn't spend a lot of time together—we
did. And I am grateful that we were actively involved in church, sports,
drama, and eating.
I do remember a lot of eating.

There was a lot of laughter and fun in our home.
It goes with the fact that most of us are sarcastically gifted.

But I do wish when it came to quality time in the evenings or weekends,
we had just played together more. Looking back now, I realize I didn't
know how much fun mattered then—and I didn't really know how to
play that well.

I did have some cues.
When my son was almost four, I remember leaving to go back to work
on a busy weekend, and he asked me this question:
"Daddy, when we get to heaven, will you have more time to play
with me?"

He definitely made his point. Not long afterwards, I took another job so
I could have more time together as a family. But learning how to *play*
was still one of my greatest problems. I would have signed up for a
class on "play" if I could have found one.

Personally, I have been extremely grateful for other adults who show up
in my kids' lives to have fun with them:
grandparents
aunts and uncles
adult friends
other kids' parents
church and school leaders

If you are one of those leaders who spends time with someone else's kid, remember that fun matters. You are helping kids build a healthy play history. And, if you leverage your influence well, you may actually have an opportunity to help families have fun together.

NOT EVERYTHING IN LIFE IS FUN. BUT YOU HAVE AN OPPORTUNITY EVERY WEEK TO MAKE SOMETHING FUN. HERE ARE JUST A FEW OF THE IDEAS I WISH SOMEONE HAD SHARED WITH ME WHEN I WAS YOUNGER.

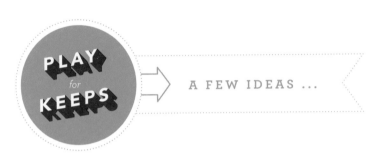

A FEW IDEAS ...

LOOSEN UP

Again, some of us have a serious issue with taking ourselves too seriously. That's why one of the first things you can do to make every week more fun is to let go of a few things like your
Image
Ego
Pride

YOU HAVE AN OPPORTUNITY EVERY
WEEK TO SHOW KIDS AND TEENAGERS
YOU CARE MORE ABOUT THEM THAN
WHAT OTHER PEOPLE THINK ABOUT
YOU. YOU SHOW THEM YOU CARE
WHEN YOU ALLOW YOURSELF TO BE
VULNERABLE ENOUGH TO JUST HAVE
FUN. **SO LOOSEN UP.**

LOOSEN UP THIS WEEK BY MOVING MORE.

Literally. Move. Maybe one of the reasons adults have "lost that playing feeling" is because we spend too much time sitting still. According to Stuart Brown, "If you're having a bad day, jump up and down—you will feel better." Jumping activates your play drive. So, maybe you should make random jumping your go-to solution when you can't think of anything else to do.

There's also a lot to be said for dancing, running, riding a bike, and other activities that put your body in motion.

YOU CAN ALSO LOOSEN UP BY LAUGHING MORE.

Laughter is the universal language. Everybody immediately knows what laughter means—it means somebody is having fun. When you laugh together, it means you enjoy being together.

Some experts think laughter may actually be the quickest and most effective way to connect. According to Regina Barreca, Ph.D., "Laughing together is as close as you can get to a hug without touching."[8]

SO HOW MUCH LAUGHTER HAPPENS IN YOUR HOME OR CHURCH?

OF COURSE, ONE OF THE MOST OBVIOUS WAYS TO LOOSEN UP IS TO PLAY MORE.

Play will never feel urgent in your weekly schedule. If you are a leader, you're probably more concerned with how you will communicate content than you are with how you will play. If you are a parent, you're probably more concerned with things like laundry, dinner, homework, and discipline than play. That's why you have to plan for it.

In his book *Playful Parenting*, Lawrence Cohen encourages parents to "Make a conscious transition from work—or whatever else you're doing—to play: Change into play clothes. Set a timer for half an hour or an hour. During this time, give your child 100 percent of your attention—no phone calls, no preparing dinner."[9]

As leaders and parents, set aside time just to play.

One more thing about loosening up—
Sometimes you won't feel like it. You may be tired, frustrated, or
stressed, and the idea of laughing, moving, and playing will seem like
the last thing you can imagine doing. Fun doesn't have to be a feeling.
But when you choose to have fun and loosen up in spite of your
feelings, you may end up actually feeling a lot more fun than
you thought.

LEARN WHAT THEY LIKE

If you want to make something fun, it has to be fun for them.
Okay, that's pretty intuitive.

Sometimes as leaders and parents, we make the assumption that
because they are younger, kids and teenagers are the ones who should
be learning from us. But creating a playful and engaging atmosphere
is critical for learning. So, if you really want them to learn, you need to
learn what they like.

You need to . . .
Tune in to their laughter. If they are laughing, it's a good clue about
what they think is fun.

Let them choose. You don't have to plan an extravagant "fun night"
in order to have fun. Sometimes the best thing you can do is make
yourself available. Then, let them lead you.

Listen to their stories. Kids and teenagers may not begin many
conversations with "I like . . ." (if they do, that would be a pretty good

clue about what they like). But if you listen to the stories they tell, you can pick up some ideas about what they enjoy or don't enjoy doing.

JUST REMEMBER . . .

THEY MAY NOT KNOW WHAT THEY LIKE.
This is especially true for younger kids. Five-year-olds may not know yet that they like Candy Land, baseball, or Marco Polo—until you play with them.

WHAT YOU LIKE MAY NOT BE WHAT THEY LIKE.
This is especially true if you're trying to have fun with teenagers. They have already discovered their own style of fun. And what they are still discovering may be more fun for them if they discover it first. So, make sure you don't force them to play on your terms.

WHAT THEY LIKE MAY NOT BE WHAT YOU LIKE.
Stretch a little. You're the adult. Learning what they like may involve learning to do something you wouldn't otherwise love to do. But you do it because you love them, and you want to make it fun.

LOSE THE AGENDA

As parents and leaders, you will probably always have an agenda.
You want them to . . .
be polite,
love God,
make good grades,
know their memory verse.

If you're honest, the agenda list is a really long list. It gets shorter as
they get older because you just start prioritizing for the big stuff . . .
Don't smoke.
Don't get pregnant.
Only drive when you're sober.
(Of course your list will never look like that. You have good kids.)

NO MATTER HOW LONG OR HOW
URGENT THE AGENDA IS, THERE MAY BE
A TIME WHEN YOU HAVE TO CHOOSE TO
SET IT ASIDE FOR THE SAKE OF FUN.

I (Kristen) remember a few years ago when I was leading a small group and one of the girls had stopped attending. I knew she was making some unwise choices related to drinking, and she was choosing not to come to church anymore because she didn't want to feel judged for her decisions. But here's the interesting thing: she still liked hanging out. She and I would meet from time to time, at Starbucks, at a school event, at a retreat—anywhere that she knew we would have *fun*. And in those moments, I didn't talk about her decisions. She knew what I thought. Sometimes she would bring it up, and we would talk about it. But I knew at that juncture in her life, it was more important to have fun and stay connected than to continue reminding her of something she already knew.

We aren't suggesting that fun is more important than rules, or that it outweighs instruction. Kids and teenagers need those things, too. (Remember, we talked about that in the Love Over Time chapter.) We are just saying there may also be times when it's more important to value the relationship by having fun together.

If you're a parent, you may need to set aside time with your kids when you agree not to discuss their issues. This can be especially true if they are in a tough season of life. When the tension is high, you need a scheduled break—just to have fun together.

HINT

MOST KIDS AND TEENAGERS SHUT DOWN WHEN YOU TAKE THE EYE-TO-EYE, "LET'S TALK ABOUT WHAT'S GOING ON" APPROACH. THEY TEND TO TALK MORE WHEN THEY'RE ENGAGED IN A FUN ACTIVITY, NOT MAKING EYE CONTACT, AND FEEL IN CONTROL OF THE AGENDA.

That's just one reason we believe church should be fun—every week. If you're a leader, it should be a part of every aspect of what you do. Because you are a Christian, right?

Howard Hendricks, a former professor at Dallas Theological Seminary, said, "It's a sin to bore a child with the Word of God."

So . . .
Crank up the music.
Be creative with the video.
Find some engaging personalities to communicate.
Plan to laugh a lot in your circle.

Just get serious about having some fun,
if you want kids and teenagers to get serious about what matters.

NEHEMIAH SAID,
"THE JOY OF THE LORD IS
YOUR STRENGTH."
IF THAT IS TRUE,
HOW STRONG IS YOUR CHURCH?
HOW STRONG IS YOUR HOME?[10]

It's not that fun is the most important thing. But if you don't have fun, little else matters. If you love kids, but you don't play with them, they may not feel like you like them.

If you give teenagers words and stories that are boring, they may not care. If you belog to a tribe that never laughs, they won't want to be a part of it.

So whatever you do this week, make it fun.

If you want to
build trust. . .
have lasting influence. . .
establish a deeper connection. . .
you have to make fun a priority.

FUN OVER TIME
IS ONE OF THE
BEST WAYS TO CONNECT
TO THE HEART OF
A KID OR TEENAGER.

MAKE IT
FUN

From the Losing Your Marbles story

BETWEEN THE LINES

THINK ABOUT

DIANE

Diane leads a full life. As a nurse practitioner and the single mother of a middle-schooler, it's admirable that she is able to keep the bills paid, the laundry done, and food on the table. She works long hours and could easily come home too tired for fun—but she doesn't.

Diane makes life fun.

In fact, Diane compromises on some of the non-essentials in order to make fun essential. Her house isn't spotless. Her laundry is folded—on the kitchen chair. And you might have to move a stack of magazines and pre-approved credit card mailers if you want to sit on the sofa.

From the Losing Your Marbles story

BETWEEN THE LINES

But when Diane sits down to a dinner of Simon's favorite take-out, she is ready for fun. She incorporates games into everyday routines. She doesn't take herself too seriously. She is attentive to her son's emotions and stays interested. And she even lets Simon choose what and how they will play—most of the time.

Maybe that's why Simon
trusts,
respects,
and enjoys being around her.

Diane has a deeper connection with her son because she has made fun one of her family values. Over time, she has leveraged fun to make home the kind of place Simon wants to be now, and the kind of place he will want to come back to after he leaves.

MAKE IT
FUN

KNUCKLE DOWN:

Write the name of each kid or teenager in your circle of influence. What are some things you can think of that each one likes? (You might want to check it with them. They may have changed their minds since last week.)

MAKE IT
FUN

**WHAT YOU DO TO MAKE THIS WEEK FUN
FOR A KID OR TEENAGER MATTERS.**

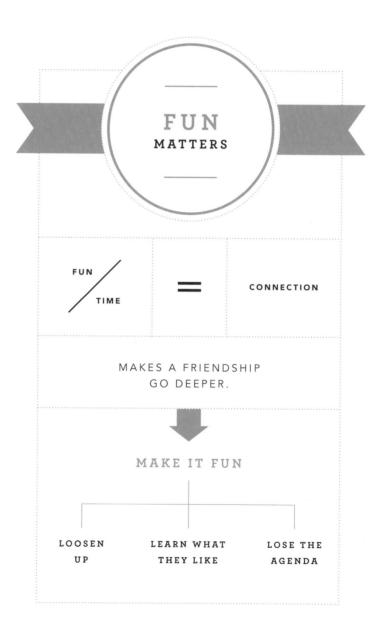

FUN
MATTERS

FUN / TIME = CONNECTION

MAKES A FRIENDSHIP
GO DEEPER.

↓

MAKE IT FUN

| LOOSEN UP | LEARN WHAT THEY LIKE | LOSE THE AGENDA |

WHATEVER
MATTERS WILL
MATTER
EVEN MORE

OVER TIME

WE WROTE THIS BOOK FOR ONE SIMPLE REASON:

WHAT YOU DO FOR KIDS OVER TIME MATTERS.

One of the reasons we know that's true is because what you *don't* do for kids over time matters. We could have written several chapters about what happens when children and teenagers don't get

TIME	LOVE	WORDS
STORIES	TRIBES	FUN

OVER TIME.

The absence of those things in someone's life can have powerfully negative consequences. Our culture is full of people who struggle because they were rejected, abused, isolated, neglected, or abandoned.

That's why what you do every week can actually give kids a better sense of worth, belonging, connection, direction, and perspective.

If it takes time over time to make history,
then it takes love, words, stories, tribes, and fun over time
to make a history that's worth repeating.

JUST REMEMBER . . .

TIME

LOVE

WORDS

STORIES

TRIBES

FUN

WILL NEVER MEAN MUCH WITHOUT TIME.

Love without time is just infatuation.
Words without time are just nouns and verbs.
Tribes without time are just familiar faces.
Fun without time is just a game.
Stories without time are just incidental.

But when you give these things to a kid or teenager *over time,* they do something transformational.

THINK ABOUT IT THIS WAY.

LOVE IS JUST LOVE.

It's a second-hand emotion—
until you put it over time.

Then it does something amazing.
It gives a kid **WORTH**.

WORDS ARE JUST SOMETHING TO HELP YOU WIN AT SCRABBLE®.

They're something you tweet to get more followers—
until you put them over time.

Then, they become a collection of messages
that moves someone in a better **DIRECTION**.

STORIES ARE JUST EXPERIENCES THAT HAPPEN TO HAVE HAPPENED

unless Spielberg produces one, and it gets an Oscar.

But when you collect stories over time,
they expand a child's imagination
in a way that can shape his or her **PERSPECTIVE**.

TRIBES ARE JUST PEOPLE LINKED TOGETHER BY COMMON INTERESTS.

They're clubs you can sign up to attend—
until you put them over time.

Then they become a family or community
where a child can expeience **BELONGING**.

....

FUN IS JUST A GOOD TIME.

It's fun, period, just an Indie pop band—
until you put it over time.

Then it creates a powerful **CONNECTION**.
It takes your friendship with a teenager deeper.

....

What you are doing every week will matter more in someone's life
when you do it . . .
week after week,
month after month,
year after year.

And when you combine love, words, stories, fun, and tribes together
over time . . .
they gain collective momentum.
they make history.
they build a legacy.

DON'T MISS THIS:
WHATEVER MATTERS WILL
MATTER EVEN MORE
OVER TIME.

It pays to keep doing what you do.

That's why . . .

. . . pastors who stay at a church for several years encounter a different kind of response from people.

. . . leaders who work with the same kid or teenager for multiple seasons experience a different kind of influence.

. . . parents who engage with sons and daughters through every stage of life enjoy a different kind of relationship.

That's also why some wine, steak, and cheese just tastes better.

Some things can only happen over time.

So, what you do this week matters.
It matters because every week is one in a number of weeks.
And the weeks add up.

Sure, there are nearly a **thousand weeks between birth and graduation.** But they go by fast.

So remember:
You will only know a child as a six-year-old once—
then he or she will be seven.

That may not seem like a very profound statement now, but one day it will.

This week is a moment in time when you can step into their world and know them for who they are right now.

Next year at this time, they will have changed.
And you will have played a role in that change.

You're playing for keeps.
So visit their world as many times as you can this week, and keep doing what you do.

PLAY A GAME.
TELL THEM A STORY.
GIVE THEM A TRIBE.
SAY IT AGAIN.
AND PROVE YOU LOVE THEM.
AGAIN AND AGAIN.

BECAUSE OVER TIME,

IT MATTERS.

MORE RESOURCES

Legacy Marbles Resources
www.LosingYourMarblesBook.com

Parenting Beyond Your Capacity:
Connect Your Family to a Wider Community
By Reggie Joiner, Carey Nieuwhof (David C Cook, 2010)

Orange Parents Blog
www.OrangeParents.org

Lead Small:
Five Big Ideas Every Small Group Leader Needs to Know
By Reggie Joiner, Tom Shefchunas (The reThink Group, 2012)

Lead Small Blog
www.LeadSmall.org

Parent CUE App
Legacy Countdown App
available for iPhone and android

Orange
www.ThinkOrange.com

Studio 252
www.Studio252.tv

Follow the conversation
#losingyourmarbles

WHO WE ARE

REGGIE JOINER

Reggie is the founder and CEO of The reThink Group, a nonprofit organization providing resources and training to help churches maximize their influence on the spiritual growth of the next generation. He is one of the founding pastors of North Point Community Church in Alpharetta, Ga. In his role as the executive director of Family Ministry, Reggie led a team to develop concepts of ministry for preschoolers, children, students, and married adults over the course of his 11 years with the church. He is the author of *Think Orange* and his latest books include *Parenting Beyond Your Capacity; Slow Fade; Lead Small;* and *Zombies, Football and the Gospel.* Reggie and Debbie live in Cumming, Ga., and have four grown children: Reggie Paul, Hannah, Sarah, and Rebekah.

ELIZABETH HANSEN

Elizabeth Hansen is a writer and story developer for Orange with a graduate degree in script and screenwriting. She and her husband, David, produce promotional and narrative films through their production company, Arclight Studios. Like Diane, she is a Scrabble® fiend. And like Simon, she is fond of hatching plots.

KRISTEN IVY

Kristen Ivy combines her degree in secondary education with a Master of Divinity to help churches re-think the way they practice spiritual formation, education, and discipleship for the next generation. She is the director of messaging for Orange and has played a role in launching XP3 Students, CUE Box, and Studio 252. Kristen lives out the full Orange spectrum as the wife of XP3 Students Orange Specialist Matt Ivy, and the mother of two First-Look (preschool) children, Sawyer and Hensley.

ABBY JARTOS

Abby Jartos picked up the crayons early and never looked back, and now loves to draw pictures all day at her home outside Atlanta. Her work helps tell stories in a variety of formats and media. Visit her online at www.abbyjartos.com.

WORKS CITED

Time Over Time

[1] Trace Adkins. Just Fishin (Nashville: Show Dog Universal Music, 2011).

Love Over Time

[1] Matt 22:37-39. RJLT (Reggie Joiner's Loose Translation.)

[2] Sue Gerhardt, *Why Love Matters: How Affection Shapes a Baby's Brain* (New York: Routledge, 2004), 83.

[3] Gerhardt, *Why Love Matters*, 89

[4] World Health Organization. Early Childood Development: A Powerful Equalizer. Final Report. 2007, 5. http://www.who.int/social_determinants/resources/ecd_kn_report_07_2007.pdf (24 Mar. 2013)

Word Over Time

[1] A quick note about "Words" for those of you who are thorough enough to read the footnotes: For the purpose of simplifying this chapter, we didn't define what we mean by words. However, it's important to mention that a word in its simplest sense doesn't have to be spoken or heard to exist. There are countless individuals who have extensive unspoken vocabularies. It's our opinion that these words are as significant as those we speak and hear.

[2] Lera Boroditsky, "Lost in Translation," *The Wall Street Journal*, (July 23, 2010), accessed March 27, 2013, http://online.wsj.com/article/SB100014240527487034673045753831315927 67868.html

[3] ibid.

[4] E.D. Hirsch, Jr., "Vocabulary Declines with Unspeakable Results," *The Wall Street Journal*, (December 12, 2012), accessed March 27, 2013, http://online.wsj.com/article/SB100008723 963904441658045780103942786884 54.html

Stories Over Time

[1] Liisa Ogburn, "Why Use Story?" *We are Wired for Stories*, accessed April 1, 2013, http://www.WiredForStories.com.

[2] J.K. Rowling in her Harvard Commencement address, "The Fringe Benefits of Failure and the Importance of Imagination," *Harvard Magazine*, June 5, 2008.

[3] Keith Oatley, "Fiction Hones Social Skills," *Scientific American*, November 20, 2011.

[4] J.K. Rowling, "The Fringe Benefits of Failure and the Importance of Imagination."

[5] Katherine Hankey, "I Love to Tell the Story, " lyrics written in 1866, (no 626) in the *Baptist Hymnal*, (Nashville, TN: Lifeway Worship, 2008).

SIMON
is trying to rescue a
friend and resolve a question
he's had his entire life.

MAX
is hoping to find
somewhere to belong.

ERIC
is searching for a
reason to matter.

KEN
is helping kids discover a
secret about their future.

MARCUS
is looking for a way back
into his son's life.

DIANE
is learning how to let go.

They all have one thing in common.

Time is running out.

Losing Your Marbles

Published by Orange, a division of The reThink Group, Inc.
5870 Charlotte Lane, Suite 300
Cumming, GA 30040 U.S.A.

The Orange logo is a registered trademark of The reThink Group, Inc.

All Scripture quotations, unless otherwise noted, are taken from the Holy Bible, New International Version®. NIV®. Copyright © 1973, 1978, 1984 by International Bible Society. Used by permission of Zondervan.

Other Orange products are available online and direct from the publisher. Visit our website at www.WhatIsOrange.org for more resources like these.

ISBN: 978-0-9854116-9-5

©2013 Reggie Joiner

Writers: Reggie Joiner, Elizabeth Hansen, Kristen Ivy
Lead Editor: Karen Wilson
Editors: Mike Jeffries, Cara Martens, Jennifer Wilder
Art Direction: Ryan Boon
Illustrator: Abby Jartos
Design: FiveStone

Printed in the United States of America
First Edition 2013

1 2 3 4 5 6 7 8 9 10

04/16/13

LOSING YOUR MARBLES

A LOT CAN HAPPEN
IN A WEEK

REGGIE JOINER   **ELIZABETH HANSEN**   **KRISTEN IVY**
Illustrator: **ABBY JARTOS**

orange

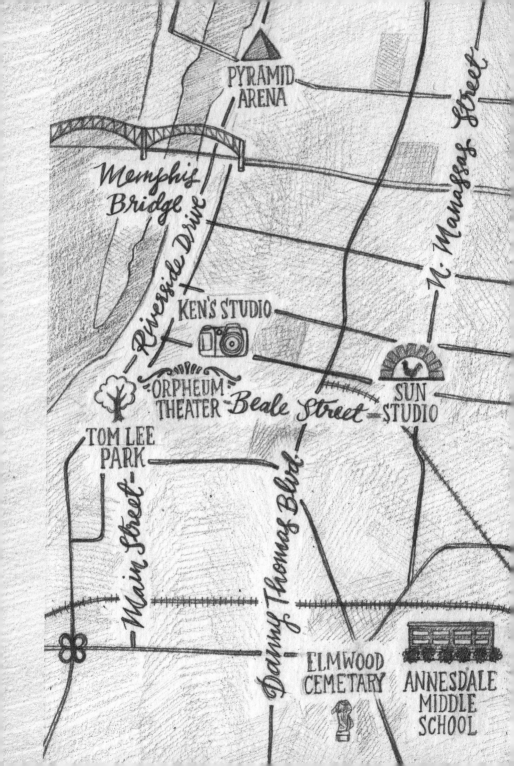

"Right now every second was vital."

FRIDAY

Simon Smith slammed his locker shut. He slung his backpack over his shoulder and glanced up at the clock on the wall. It read 3:05, but Simon didn't trust it. Not completely. Right now every second was vital.

Taking advantage of his small size, he slipped quickly between students in the emptying halls of Annesdale Middle School. The lockers were still new and shiny, but the concrete floors and rugged brick walls were reminders that the public charter school had been an abandoned warehouse just three years ago.

"Watch it, Curly Cue!" shouted a greasy-faced seventh grader flanked on both sides by giggling girls. Simon hardly noticed the fruit of their labor: a ceiling tile carefully studded with #2 pencils. He smiled apologetically as he picked up the pace. There was no time for this. Not now.

Simon checked his phone: 3:07. *He had only three minutes to reach Max Matthews.*

Striding around the corner, Simon skidded to a halt. There in his path stood the one person he didn't need right now: Nick Darby.

An eighth grader, Nick was smooth and confident in everything he did. To teachers, he was a golden boy who aced his classes and had recently pitched the first no-hitter in school history. Only his classmates saw the torment he regularly inflicted on the school's underdogs. Right now, Nick was focused on sixth-grader James Merona. It was clear that Nick had filched James' new 35-millimeter camera.

"Look what we have here, Jimmy," Nick drawled. "Nice camera. I might even let you use it once in a while . . . for a small fee."

Simon was pretty sure James would rather lose an arm than the camera he'd saved up for all year. But before Simon could step in, the school's French teacher, Madame Mince, walked briskly up the hallway. Instantly, Nick draped his arm around the younger boy's shoulders, charm oozing from his stark white smile.

"Bonjour, Madame!" Nick said smoothly, and the teacher's face lit up. "Your pronunciation is impeccable, Monsieur Darby," she announced.

Two minutes to find Max. Simon's stomach churned. He knew Nick had a pre-arranged meeting with Max at 3:10. Simon could wait and follow Nick after this little diversion, but it was crucial to reach Max first.

Leaving the drama behind, Simon sprinted the opposite direction. He could circle around the History hall and still reach the library first. It wasn't an original place for a secret meeting, but Nick liked to consider himself an intellectual, carrying around books like *The Odyssey* that Simon knew he never opened.

With another burst of speed, Simon hurtled down the hall and made two quick turns. Sure enough, there was Max—halfway to the library door, his backpack slipping off his shoulder.

"Max!" Simon called out in a strained whisper, just loud enough

to reach the younger boy's ears.

Max jerked around, his stocky frame tense. The blood drained from his face, leaving it pasty and flat underneath his mop of sweaty, dark hair. "Hey, Smith," Max squeaked, his voice betraying him. But Simon wasn't tempted to laugh; Nick and his cohort Brody couldn't be far away.

Simon took a breath to steady his own voice. "You don't have to do it."

"Do what?" Max's backpack hit the scuffed floor, landing with a dull thud between them. He started to reach for it. Then— as if stooping would put him at a disadvantage—simply pushed it against the wall with his foot.

Simon lowered his voice. "I heard them at lunch—Nick and Brody. I know they want you to help them hack into the grades database. They're trouble."

"None of your business who I hang out with," Max glowered.

"Yeah, well they want you to make me help, too. Right?" Simon pressed. "That makes it my business."

"C'mon." Max tried to laugh it off. "It's just for fun. You're good at all that tech stuff. You help do it, and he . . . we . . . we'll cut you in on the profits."

"What if I don't?" Simon kept his tone level. Max fed on even the smallest dregs of approval. He wanted acceptance from the ringleaders of this operation, but he craved approval from Simon, too—even though Simon barely ranked in the twisted hierarchy of middle school.

"Nick has friends in high school," Max muttered, shooting a nervous glance down the hallway. "They can help him get ahold of

. . . well, stuff the teachers could find in your locker. Stuff you don't want them finding. If you don't help."

There was no need for blackmail, Simon thought. Max was enough reason for Simon to get involved. Recently, he had unearthed a secret about Max that no one else knew—not even Max. Simon wanted to keep an eye on him. But it seemed like Max might already be in too deep for Simon's help.

Simon could feel the seconds ticking away. Time. He needed more time.

"I need time," he said firmly. "To research the database."

"Nick won't wait. You'd better figure it out fast, or he'll make sure my dad—I mean, Mr. Matthews—finds something in your locker."

"So old school." Simon fixed Max with an even stare, adding, "Why wouldn't Nick just trash my Facebook wall instead?"

"I don't know what you mean." Unnerved, Max grabbed his backpack and slung it over his shoulder, but Simon continued to stare him down. Over the past few months, a Facebook profile by the name of AMS Reaper had wreaked havoc on the walls of Annesdale Middle students. Taunts were plastered side-by-side with humiliating photos and even video. AMS Reaper walked a fine line, pushing kids to the point of red-faced shame, but not into telling their parents.

"Fine." Simon sighed. Mr. Matthews, the principal, was Max's father. And above all things, Simon did not want Mr. Matthews involved.

Max was breathing quickly now, eyes darting in all directions as he searched for Nick. Simon knew he would have to try again later if he didn't want Max to be swept up in Nick's latest scheme.

"See you Monday, then," Simon said and turned away quickly to end the conversation. But a few steps down the hall, he stopped and glanced back to spy Max's mop of dark hair disappearing into the library.

Simon doubled back. He had no scruples about listening in when the stakes were so high. As he feared, Nick was making short work of Max, just inside the room.

"That's it. First, get the key. And we gotta have the Smith kid to work out the code. He's your friend, right?"

"I . . . uh . . . yeah . . . ," Max stumbled.

As far as Simon could tell, Max hadn't made *any* friends in Memphis yet. Nick and Brody sure didn't count.

"Good. You get Smith," Nick ordered.

"I just need . . . more time," Max stammered.

Simon winced. Max was an easy target.

"Shut it," growled Brody. "You'll make it happen before the PTA circus next Friday. We gotta be up and running by finals."

Simon calculated quickly. The PTA always did a barbecue fundraiser at the beginning of May, when the citywide Memphis in May festivities started. The whole neighborhood would be enticed by the smells of pork falling off the bone, the tang of vinegar mixed with brown sugar and cayenne. The school itself would be wide open.

"That's only a week away!" Max squeaked from inside the library.

"The kid can do math!" Simon heard Brody mock.

Simon jumped as, without warning, the library door flung open. Skidding quickly around the corner of the hall, he plastered himself against the wall and inched back to peek around the corner. Nick and Brody sauntered out and disappeared. Max followed, slowed by a heavy weight of dread.

Simon started to call out, but before the sound left his throat, Mr. Matthews entered the hall from the opposite direction. Max flushed, but set his jaw in defiance.

"Max!" Mr. Matthews strode down the hall and placed a hand on his son's shoulder. "I'm leaving early. I'll give you a ride home."

Max fixed his eyes on the floor, but Simon studied Mr. Matthews. The older man's springy curls seemed to carry their own energy, just like his eyes—always in motion, never missing the obscene gesture under the desk, the phone pulled out for a text during class.

Simon could only pray Mr. Matthews wasn't as perceptive when it came to his son. Or Simon.

The phone in Simon's pocket vibrated. He leaned back against the wall and reached into his pocket. But his fingers slid past the phone and touched a round glass marble, pitted with age. His hand closed tightly around it.

Simon allowed the phone to keep ringing as he spotted the clock on the opposite wall. 3:37. He was late for his drum lesson. But it would be his mom calling, rather than his drumming instructor. Eric would be irritated if Simon made him waste time waiting around. But like any high school senior, he wouldn't call.

★ ★ ★

Less than half a mile away, Eric Rogers stared out the kitchen window as his father's fingers thumped the keys of his laptop. Eric had heard Marcus abuse computer keyboards for eighteen years, but was still surprised sometimes the keys didn't just give up and quit.

Behind them, the KitchenAid beaters churned, radiating Lisa's disapproval. Eric's mother was working hard to channel her frustration into the red velvet cake batter instead of her son. "*Trespassing*, Eric?" she pleaded. "Just give us one reason not to ground you for the rest of the school year."

"School year?" Marcus muttered. Shaking his head, he punched the "delete" key, destroying a whole paragraph of text. Marcus trained and polished every word he wrote for the newspaper—but his spoken words never came so easily.

Eric studied the abandoned warehouses down the street and tried to imagine what they would look like next year, crowded with upscale condos. Since that's what they would be, according to Marcus' ever-so-fascinating revelations about his most recent real estate articles.

"I'm not going to college," Eric reminded them. He hoped this was enough to sidetrack Lisa from her current hysterics.

The KitchenAid spattered and died abruptly. Lisa dabbed at specks of red cake batter splattered across her polished white kitchen tiles. "Oh, Eric! You promised. You said you'd register for classes at Southwest before graduation."

Lisa was brilliant at taking Eric's words and translating them to suit her own hopeful ideas. Eric wondered if she fed them through a special app in her brain.

Please translate: "Sure. Southwest doesn't entirely suck."

Thank you, Lisa. Interpretation complete: "Mom, I will register for classes at Southwest immediately."

Actually, Eric *had* considered community college—until Bill, his boss at The Memphis Drum Shop, offered to promote him to full-time hours. Talking drums all day and playing music at night . . . how could he pass that up?

"Eric, are you listening?" Lisa's voice was exasperated, and Eric realized she'd been talking. "You think it's no big deal, breaking into Annesdale Mansion, waking up the neighborhood?"

She was back on track, determined to glean even an ounce of genuine remorse from her son for his actions. But just like so many of Lisa's impassioned crusades, this was a hopeless battle. Eric didn't see how any harm had been done. He and Israel had simply climbed to the roof of the abandoned home, with his *djembe* and Israel's bass, to put on a little neighborhood show. They'd hardly "woken up the neighborhood."

"It's not like anyone lives there," he pointed out.

"It's private property," Marcus said as he stopped typing to scrawl notes on a yellow legal pad.

Eric resented every word his parents forced from him. Why was an explanation even necessary? Where was Simon? If that kid would just show up for his drum lesson, Eric would have an out already.

"The cop let us play for twenty minutes before making us come down. We had a good crowd." Eric silently congratulated himself on one of his best publicity stunts yet. The notoriety was sure to bolster turnout for Wednesday's concert.

"My tax dollars at work," grumbled Marcus.

Lisa attacked the batter with a spatula, scooping it into the spring form pan she always used when baking cakes for entertaining. "That does not excuse trespassing," she snapped as she shoved the cake in the oven. Setting the timer, she whipped into her clean-up routine and glanced back at Eric. "We have one hour. Is that what you're wearing for dinner?"

"Dinner?" Eric had completely forgotten, or mentally blocked, their earlier conversation. Dinner with the Eggers was one of Lisa's latest inventions for inspiring Eric to make something of himself. The Eggers' daughter Kathleen would be graduating in the top ten percent of the class. She was Student Government, Beta Club, and National Honor Society all in one. She applied to "real" universities and was accepted to everything early-admission—the perfect example of what Marcus and Lisa had hoped Eric would become.

"I'm not going," Eric said, bracing for the storm. He knew he was already on thin ice. But dinner with the Eggers wasn't going to help.

"They're expecting all three of us! Your father came home early."

"I still have to submit this article by six," Marcus warned, thumbing through a tattered pocket dictionary.

Eric smirked at the text in his father's hands. "You know, they've got this thing called the Internet now."

"There's more than one way to expand your vocabulary," Marcus retorted through tight lips.

"Please." Lisa's voice was edging up the scale, which meant she was trying not to cry. "We'd just like to have dinner with you for once this week."

For a moment, Eric considered giving in. He knew his mother was worried about him. But she was worried for the wrong reasons.

Dinner with Kathleen wasn't going to change his mind, and he had no language to convince her he was fine.

"Honey, the Eggers are such nice people and . . . ," Lisa glanced at her husband for help, but Marcus had switched to his thesaurus, still searching for the perfect adjective. "Marcus?" she pleaded.

Marcus glanced from his wife's exasperated face to Eric, and once more at the thesaurus in his hand. It never seemed to have the words he really needed, anyway. "You won't go to the Eggers. You won't go to college. You're going nowhere," he said quietly.

Eric gritted his teeth. Unlike Lisa, Marcus never yelled. Instead, his matter-of-fact criticisms were filed away in Eric's memory.

"You don't have an ounce of motivation."
"You're irrational."
"Idealistic."
"You're going nowhere."

Sometimes Eric felt his father viewed him as just another real estate venture, something to be written up and critiqued.

"*The Flyer* called Bright Midnight the top young indie group to watch in Memphis," Eric pointed out, trying to hold back the hurt in his voice.

"*The Flyer* is second-rate trash."

"Why, because they gave me a good review? At least I know what I want. And I'm doing it!"

Despite steamy heat from the oven, the air in the kitchen seemed to freeze. It was no secret that Marcus hated his job: editing the real estate section of Memphis' only daily newspaper. He had once been a musician like Eric. Now the music scene only reminded

him of the monotony of his present life.

Defeated, Lisa sank into a seat beside her husband. "I'm sure the Eggers will understand."

For a long moment the only sound in the kitchen was the clicking of Marcus' keyboard—and Lisa's unspoken hope that somehow Eric might change his mind about dinner, about college, about life.

"Well, then," Lisa spoke into the tension that filled the room. "With you working all day tomorrow, I guess we won't see you much until church on Sunday."

Eric sighed. She was trying. "I don't know," he muttered, the staid hymns and monotone sermon already trudging through his brain.

But Marcus had heard enough. He clicked "send" and closed his laptop with relief. "Well, I do know. After that . . . that stunt you pulled, as long as you're under this roof, you'll be in church every Sunday. Clear?"

Eric felt the anger crawling from his gut, clawing its way up his throat. It would choke him in a moment.

He turned back to the window. There was Simon, hurrying down the sidewalk. Eric tamped down his fury and turned back to his parents, expressionless.

"Gotta go. Simon's here for his lesson."

* * *

Simon glanced at the Rogers' brick house with its neat white

verandah. He briefly wished his mother had a green thumb like Mrs. Rogers, whose hyacinths and geraniums helped to keep the historic neighborhood association at bay. But he knew his mother Diane had enough trouble keeping the roof from leaking and the plumbing functional in their little home next door.

It was past time for his drum lesson, but Simon needed to think. Eric's hard-driving rudiments would leave no space for anything in his brain but strokes and rolls and paradiddles. Instead, Simon headed down the sidewalk for the stretch of cracked pavement outside a crumbling warehouse—not so different from the one his school now inhabited.

Simon's sharp eyes picked out the remains of the last chalk circle he'd drawn on the concrete. He recovered an end of chalk from his cache in a rusted-out drain spout and carefully redrew the circle. Then he released three marbles inside the lines, their bright stripes highlighted by the late afternoon sunlight.

Sitting back on his heels, Simon raked a hand through the curls his mother made him keep short, and tried to sort through the jumble in his head. Max. Nick. Brody.

Shaking his head, he studied the placement of each marble. An amber-colored Gooseberry sat precariously at the edge of the circle—ready for an easy knockout. A green Coreless Swirl lay just to the left of the center, and a dark-banded Indian Swirl had landed in a tiny divot. It would be difficult to dislodge.

Simon reached into his other pocket and plucked out his prized shooter marble, a Joseph's Coat. Leaning forward, knuckles to the pavement outside the circle, he tucked his thumb just behind the marble, eyes focused on the banded Indian Swirl. . . .

"Simon!"

He jerked sideways as the marble released. It spun wide by a

fraction of an inch.

"What're you doing, man? You got a lesson!" Eric loomed over him, arms folded.

Simon considered the tall boy with mahogany skin and dark, close-cropped hair, black T-shirt worn like a uniform. He wondered if Mrs. Rogers made Eric cut his hair, too, or if he just liked it that way. Most drummers Simon knew wore their hair long.

Retrieving the shooter, Simon hesitated. "Personal leave of absence?" he suggested, hoping it sounded impressive.

"Lame." Eric eyed the chalk circle skeptically, then chose a spot on the uneven pavement and sat down. "You could have texted."

Truthfully, Eric thought it was Simon's business whether he wanted to be any good at drumming or not. But anger from the confrontation with his parents still seeped through his veins. He pulled a pair of well-taped drumsticks from his back pocket and smacked a few rolls against the pavement. The staccato beats relieved some of the pressure in his chest.

"You don't get good by accident, you know." He switched up the rhythm. It felt good. Fresh. "Being a real drummer means going at it over and over again, even when you don't feel like it. It means sticking by the notes until the music sticks by you. Until it's swimming around in your blood."

Eric ended with a few flams. Caught his breath. Simon was staring at him, like he had just said something, well . . . true. Maybe he had. "You should get some real gigs," Eric told him. "At school or something."

Simon furrowed his brow, considering. Then he focused on the marbles again. Knuckled down. "I wanted to drum at church, but you gotta be in high school." He released the shooter. It flew

straight this time, knocking against the Coreless Swirl, bowling it out of the circle.

Eric tugged at a fraying piece of tape on one of his sticks and snapped it off. "I didn't think your mom was churchy."

Simon corralled his shooter marble again. "She's not. I ride my bike." He knuckled down, but Eric popped the marble out of his hand and held it up. "Marbles?" he jeered.

"Hey! Give it back." Simon lunged for his shooter, but Eric twisted away.

"Didn't kids do this like in the '50s or something? Church. Marbles. You're an odd duck, Smith."

Simon refused to reach; it was useless to try getting past Eric's longer wingspan. Instead, he eyed Eric, curious. He'd seen Eric climb into the family Camry with Mr. and Mrs. Rogers some Sunday mornings. "I thought your family went to church," he ventured.

"Yeah, Marcus and Lisa do." Eric shrugged. Lately he'd taken to calling his parents by their first names in public. One more way to prove they couldn't control him forever. "I guess I do too, for now. At least until I graduate and move out."

It was obvious to Simon that Eric wasn't eager to sit with his parents through a full month of Sunday morning services. If Simon played his cards well, perhaps he could score a win for Eric and make up for the ditched drum lesson.

Simon raised an eyebrow. "You want to get out of going? To your church, I mean."

"Yeah?" Eric's face registered disbelief as he tossed the marble high, barely catching it on the way back down.

"Simon
furrowed
his brow,
considering.
Then he
focused on
the marbles
again.
Knuckled
down."

Simon winced. Even though the Joseph's Coat had plenty of wear and tear, he didn't like to see it handled so lightly. "Give me my shooter, and I'll tell you."

"Okay. Let's hear it," Eric said as he tossed the marble back.

Simon weighed the glass sphere in his palm. He remembered years ago when his hand had been so small he could barely lift and balance the weight. Now, it fit there as if it were a part of him.

"You come to church with me instead," Simon offered carefully.

Eric laughed. "Right. How's that any better?" As far as Eric was concerned, any church was a waste of time. People dressed up to hide what they were like during the week, while they listened to some preacher in a suit spout do-good-isms. As far as Eric could tell, Jesus never dressed up. Eric could imagine Jesus hanging out at the Drum Shop, laughing with the band. . . .

Simon waved a hand for his attention. "Sorry," Eric apologized. "What?"

"I said, we're doing something different this Sunday. It's in the afternoon. My group leader likes when we bring friends . . . and we could definitely use you."

"Use me how?" Eric was instantly guarded.

"We usually make new visitors clean the bathrooms," Simon joked.

Would Sunday afternoon with a middle school kid cancel out Sunday morning in the company of his parents? Eric wasn't sure.

"You won't *have* to do anything," Simon offered, trying to read Eric's hesitation. "It would be cool to have you there."

Eric sighed. "Whatever. I'll come." But he secretly wondered what Marcus would say to this scheme.

Simon beamed. Stuck out his hand. "Deal."

Down the street, a compact Honda zipped into Simon's driveway. He could see his mom struggling out of the car, juggling an armload of papers and take-out boxes as usual. "Oops. Gotta go."

Scooping up his marbles, Simon took off without a backward glance to see if Eric was watching.

* * *

Simon knew what the trail would look like even before he opened the front door. Mail strewn across the sofa. Half a dozen lab coats in need of washing dropped on the settee in the hallway. Shoes kicked off at the kitchen door.

He had watched his mother at work. Diane, a nurse practitioner, kept her office immaculate, her movements neat and decisive, her prescriptions beautifully legible. At the hospital, everything about her spoke of order and efficiency.

But once Diane left the office, all that changed. Home was a comfortable clutter, and her conversation tended to dart in all directions. Simon wasn't surprised to enter the kitchen and discover Thai take-out in messy mounds on two plates, duck sauce dripping everywhere. Diane kissed him quickly on the cheek. "Hi sweetie! Curry for me, Pad Thai extra spicy for you." She always remembered his favorites.

Simon took the plate of noodles as his mother settled down at the table. They both reached for the box of *Balderdash* cards that lived with the collection of games next to the wall.

"Got a word?" Diane said with a smile.

"Got a word," Simon confirmed as he took the box and dropped it on the table in front of his mother. "But you go first."

Watching his mother flip through the stack of cards, Simon felt his world easing back toward equilibrium. Games were a language that always made sense. Diane had started him on *Sorry!* and *Operation* before he could read. He learned to spell on *Scrabble* and strategize with chess. And *Balderdash* had taught him to think on the fly, making up definitions for impossible words that actually existed.

"Ha!" Diane found her card and pulled it out. "Nelipot," she announced, pouring herself a glass of tea. "Is it 'excessive spending on food and drink' or 'someone who walks without shoes'?"

"Spell it," Simon requested, hoping to buy time.

"N-e-l-i-p-o-t." Diane dug into her meal with relish. Simon had never seen her say grace for a meal. She figured if there was a God, He put a lot more stock in the work she did saving lives at the hospital than empty words over the dinner table.

Simon had thanked God for his Frosted Flakes that morning. He decided that was good for the day and began slurping his noodles. "Where's the word come from?" he asked.

Diane shook her head. "Guess already." Simon took another bite because he knew she wouldn't make him talk with his mouth full. Usually, the word she chose had something to do with her day at work. But he couldn't quite make either of the definitions relate, and now she was whistling the *Jeopardy!* theme song to hurry him up.

"Okay, okay!" he laid down his fork in surrender. "Excessive spending on food and drink."

"Ha!" she pounced. "It's someone who walks without shoes."

Simon glanced back at her shoes in the kitchen door. "I should have known!" He took his red plastic playing piece and moved it backward a space on the makeshift board they'd scrawled on a cereal box; the real board was long gone.

"Not me," she shook her head. "This little girl came into the ER last week. She'd been outside on a construction lot barefoot and stepped on a roofing nail, and her parents didn't get it treated right away. We were afraid she was going to lose the whole foot, but today she was able to walk right out of the hospital on her own two feet! I picked up her case because Dr. Swenson just up and quit . . . ," she trailed off, sighing. "Which means I may need to pull some evening shifts the next week or so. I hate to leave you here by yourself."

Simon swallowed carefully. "I'll be fine mom. The Rogers are right next door."

"I'd still feel better if Aunt Cathy was closer than an hour away." A dollop of curry from Diane's spoon plopped onto the table. She sponged it off and slid the box of cards to Simon. "Word up?"

He tugged his card from where he'd hidden it at the back of the box and threw down the gauntlet. "'Concilliabule.' Is it 'one who fakes a smile' or 'a secret meeting of people who are hatching a plot'?" He grinned, showing all his teeth. He wondered if it looked as warm and authentic as the special smile Nick reserved for teachers.

"You're doing that to throw me off the scent, right?" Diane treated each word like a lab analysis. "You wouldn't smile if it was the fake smile, but you know I'd think that, so you would only smile if it wasn't the fake smile."

"Games
were a
language
that always
made
sense."

"Exactly." Simon maintained the grin and nodded sagely.

Diane balled up her napkin. "Fake smile!"
Simon smirked. "Nope. The secret meeting. Hatching a plot."

"Here I thought I was gaining ground." She moved her yellow game piece back a space, too. "Speaking of meetings, how was your drumming lesson?"

His small bubble of triumph deflated as the events of the afternoon flooded back. "I didn't go."

Diane coughed as she swallowed too quickly. "Simon, you don't skip! What were you doing?"

Simon knew he was reaching for the marble in his pocket, but the gesture was so ingrained he couldn't stop himself. "I hung out with that new kid, Max."

"Max . . . Matthews?" Diane's face was carefully blank.

Simon nodded; she must know. He rolled the shooter back and forth in his palm. For a moment, he wanted to lay it all out on the table: words, questions, marbles. But he couldn't do that. Not yet. Maybe not ever.

"Must you do that at the table?"

Simon shoved the marble back in his pocket. "You gave them to me."

"I shouldn't have. You were too young," Diane shook her head. "Four, I think. But you were so fascinated when you found all those old marbles in my drawer. You nearly choked on one of those twisty ones."

"Swirls," Simon corrected.

Diane thumped her empty tea glass down on the tabletop.

"Yes. I know. Let's just stick with other games at the table, okay? These last few months, it's all you do."

"All right, then. I'm done." Simon pushed back his chair and headed for his room.

"Good word!" she called after.

"Good word," he responded and shut the door gently. Firmly. Simon never slammed it.

Diane released a breath of frustration and reached for Simon's untouched glass of tea. Since Simon had started at Annesdale, time had flashed by at warp speed. She was missing things; she knew it.

You're a good mother, she reminded herself. Simon had everything he needed: four sturdy walls (though the archaic plumbing left something to be desired), plenty of food, a college education fund well underway. He'd always spoken freely with her about everything. But lately, she couldn't help feeling he was building a small, secret room inside himself she knew nothing about.

Would a father have a better chance of seeing inside? But she had made her decision years ago. She set down Simon's glass, empty.

* * *

Simon's room was as well ordered as his mother's office. He'd neatly arranged newspaper articles and Internet printouts on the wall over his desk: concerts with Memphis drumming greats Steve Potts and James Sexton. Even one about Eric's band. Simon still wasn't sure he wanted to be a drummer himself, but he liked the way that every note formed part of a larger a pattern, that every

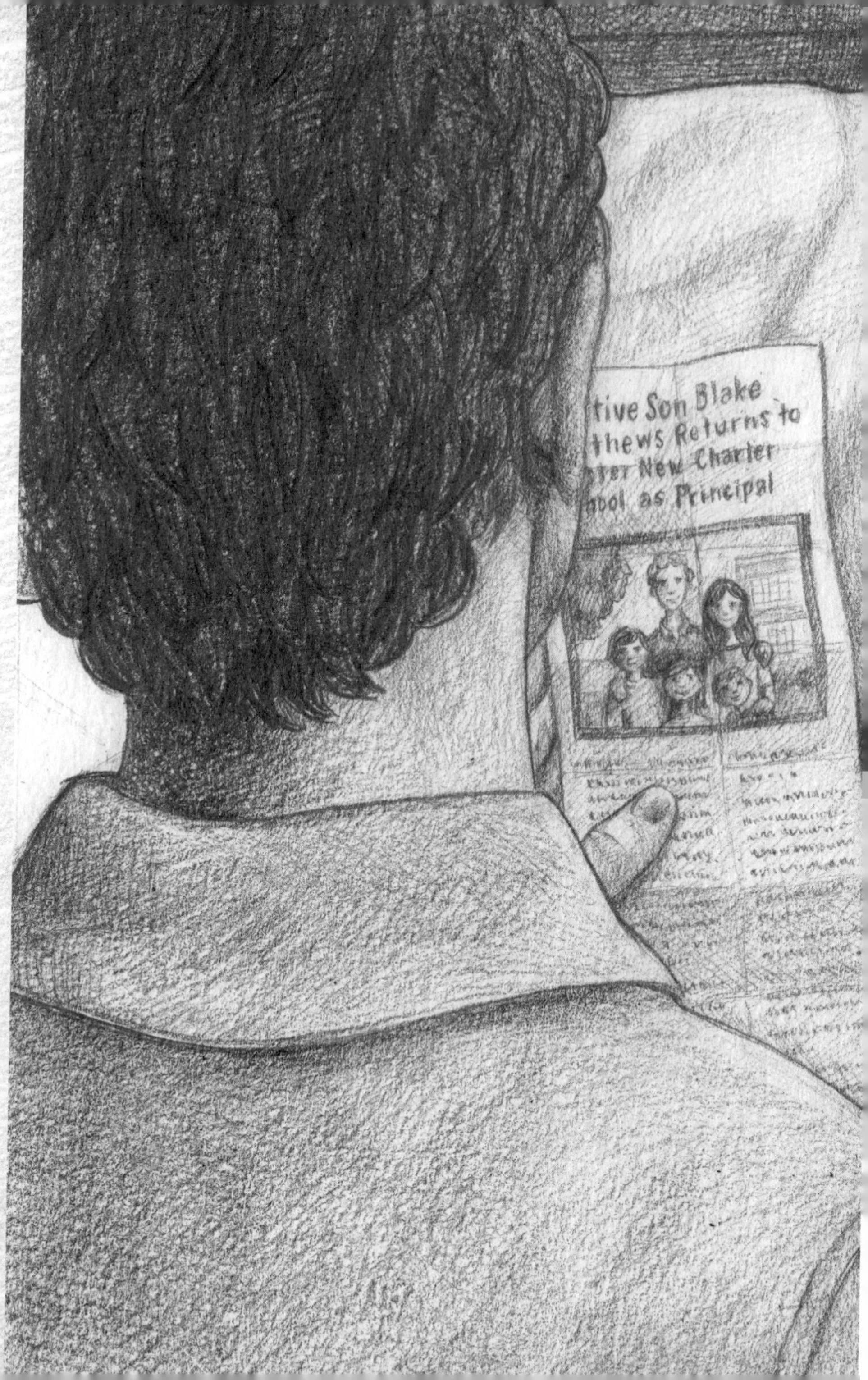
tive Son Blake
thews Returns to
New Charter
as Principal

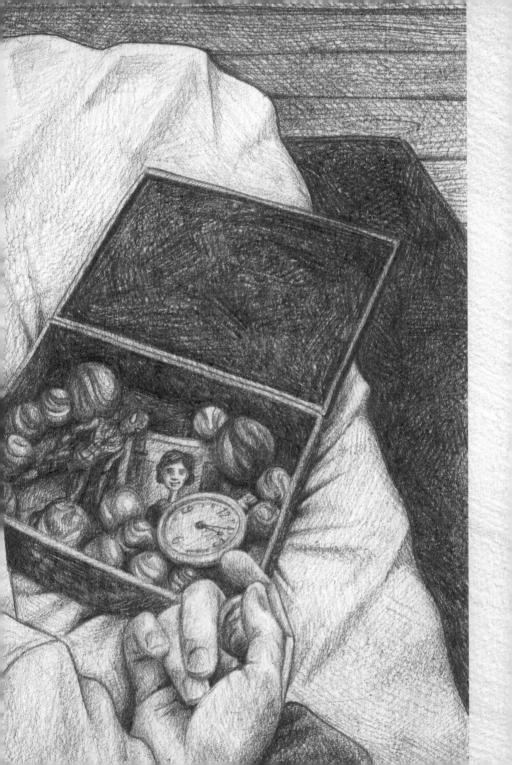

stroke meant something vital.

Kneeling, he reached under his bed and pulled out a black metal box. He'd found it years ago at a community yard sale and used it as a safe place for his marbles. But lately, he'd added other items to the collection—his group leader Ken's idea.

He opened the lid and surveyed the contents. Ken had said they should find things that would tell the story of who they were. Who he, Simon, was.

Simon had tried. There was an old black-and-white photograph of his mom's grandmother, a sweet-faced lady he remembered visiting only once. She had smelled like peppermints and cough syrup. There was a pocket watch from his mother's favorite uncle passed down from a great-great someone. There was a Spider-Man figurine his mother had bought him for his sixth birthday; Spider-Man had always been one of Simon's favorites.

And then there was Simon's marble collection. Mibs and shooters, Cat's Eyes and Bumblebees, Green Ghosts and Lutzes. The final rays of the setting sun through his window made them shine like glowing eyes: winking, watching.

Simon's favorites were still the Swirls he had found in his mother's drawer. He pulled the Joseph's Coat from his pocket and placed it beside two Latticinio marbles, one with the more traditional yellow core, the other with a rare orange center.

Simon had looked up each of his Swirls on the Internet last year and discovered their collective value could add a significant boost to his college fund. He hadn't told his mom.

Instinctively, he fished in a crevice at the edge of the box and pulled out a tightly folded newspaper clipping.

Native Son Blake Matthews Returns to Bolster New Charter

School as Principal

In a photo dated the previous August, Mr. Matthews stood with Max, two younger children, and his pale, dark-haired wife in front of Annesdale Middle.

Simon stared at the page for a long moment. Then he refolded it, tucked it back in the box, and pulled his Algebra book out of his backpack.

* * *

SATURDAY

The morning was hot for May. Eric wiped sweat from the back of his neck as he dashed off rhythms on the front porch steps. He wasn't scheduled to work for another hour.

Diggada cha chiggata dat digga doom gat!

A shout of laughter interrupted his concentration. Next door, he spotted Simon and Diane on their front porch, playing what looked like some kind of game. They did this most Saturdays, now that he thought about it.

The voices of his own parents floated through the open windows behind him.

"The *point* was to spend some more time with him!" Lisa's voice was low, tense. "Marcus, we're running out of time! It seems like yesterday he was eight and I agreed to let him have his first sleepover. Now he's 18." Lisa's voice broke off, and Eric could picture her pausing to rein in rising emotion.

Digga doom digga doom gat!

"He could decide to move out next month! How do we know he'll be okay?"

"We don't." A soft thump told Eric that Marcus had dropped down into his favorite recliner, long arms and legs sprawled in surrender. "He'll be calling his own shots soon enough. If he goes with the Smith kid . . . well, at least he's in church."

"But we don't even know . . . where does Simon go?" Lisa broke off. "Not that it matters. I only . . . we've let so much time just slide by . . . ."

Chiggata dat diggada cha—

"Eric's a good kid. He'll be okay."

Eric's wrists slackened, the drumsticks stilled. He had expected to win, in the end. But he had expected the defense to come from his mother.

A shout of victory drew his gaze back to Simon and Diane. Simon had jumped up from his seat, having clearly pulled off a stellar move. Eric couldn't help smiling; the kid threw himself completely into whatever he did, that was for sure.

★ ★ ★

From his front porch, Simon spotted Eric watching and waved. Eric didn't know it yet, but he'd have a fan club waiting tomorrow afternoon at church.

Diane raised an eyebrow at Simon across the *Risk* game board. "I hope you apologized to Eric for standing him up."

"We worked it out."

"That's good." Diane revealed a set of three playing cards. "Because—oh, look at that! Forty armies." She began triumphantly piling game tokens on Greenland and tossed him the defending dice. "Attacking Iceland with three!"

"You'll never take it," Simon rattled his dice smugly. "My guys are vets. They've been living in ice and snow for years. Your rookies don't stand a chance. And *when* I win, I'm taking all your peanut M&M's."

"No! You wouldn't," Diane exclaimed in mock horror.

"We could always switch it up and play marbles instead." Simon knew it was fruitless, but he tried anyway.

"Or *Balderdash*," Diane countered.

Simon tossed the dice. "I've got a word for you. 'Chicken!'"

"Hey," she protested, flicking an M&M at him. "I know better than to play where I'm outmatched."

Simon popped the M&M in his mouth. He wished that, just once, she'd play marbles with him anyway.

SUNDAY

Central Avenue Church blended in among its historic neighbors with soft red brick and white columns. Eric shot Simon a cynical look as he turned his battered El Camino into the parking lot. He'd been hoping for something a little different—though he wasn't sure what. Ten to one, whatever they did in this building would make him wish for a nap, despite the fact it was four in the afternoon instead of ten in the morning.

What was the point of all of it, anyway? From what Eric had picked up, Jesus taught a lot more about how to live than how to sing second-rate songs off-key. If anything, church seemed to him like one more pointless institution. Keep kids out of trouble. Keep adults in line. Make sure judgment comes swiftly for those who dare to take a different path.

Church should be on the riverfront, Eric mused. Jesus seemed to hang out a lot at the lake or down by the river. And the Mississippi could rival the Jordan River any day for thick, sticky mud.

"So, where do I park?" Eric asked, but Simon was already waving to a crowd of kids and adults milling around on the far side of the church.

"Just pull in right there by my group," Simon told him, pointing out a spot where half a dozen kids had gathered by a rickety church van. "They're the ones I meet with every week."

Simon hopped out as soon as Eric pulled in. For a moment, Eric considered backing out and fleeing. But the kids were already swarming his car. It was new for Eric, being recognized. He wanted to think it was due to his band's recent write up in *The Flyer*, but it was more likely his impromptu concert on top of Annesdale Mansion.

As Eric warily exited the car, Simon launched into introductions at top speed. Eric missed several names, but Dwayne made an impression: the kid was busy turning himself into a human pretzel. And there was Michael, a short Asian kid who managed to channel Elvis with uncanny accuracy.

"Ambition is a dream with a V8 engine," he offered in a scratchy drawl, rather than shaking Eric's hand.

A freckle-faced girl named Anna seemed out of place with her long, blond ponytail and sharp green eyes. "She's not really supposed to be part of the group," Simon explained.

Anna crossed her arms. "Yeah, well you need *someone* who can actually sing in this video," she shot back.

Eric's head was spinning. "Wait . . . what video?" A hand clapped on his shoulder, and Eric turned to face a bearded man in his forties, wearing skinny jeans and slinging a heavy camera bag. Dangerously close to hipster. In Eric's experience, the hipster brand of authenticity was just a show, like the thick-rimmed glasses—not to be trusted.

"Eric, right? I'm Ken. Simon's leader." The man held out a hand. Eric had figured out fast that you needed a strong handshake

to navigate the indie music scene. His drummer's grip usually made people back down, but Ken wasn't fazed. "Quite the coup for Simon, bringing you in."

Eric shot a glance at Simon. The kid was obviously pleased with himself. He turned back to Ken, wary. "I thought I was coming to church."

"You did." Ken smiled. "We've been talking about how everyone's life is part of a bigger story. And how we all have unique roles to play—individually and together."

"Uh, sure." Eric nodded. It kind of made sense, even if he wasn't totally sure what Ken meant by "story."

"Anyhow," Ken continued, "the middle school groups have a competition going to see who can create a music video that tells the best story. It's our '*Amp*-lify the story' challenge." Ken winced apologetically. "Yeah, I know. But we're shooting the video today, and Simon thought we could do better than a karaoke soundtrack—"

"So you can lay down a drum track for us later, right?" Simon jumped in. "But you gotta see what we do first."

The kid had nerve, Eric had to admit. But Eric wasn't about to make it easy for him. "I don't just 'lay down a track.' I need a studio."

"Ken's got one." Simon replied, smug.

Ken shook his head. "My studio is for photography. But I can get us a few hours in Denton Crump's recording studio."

Eric blinked, surprised, as Ken rose several notches in his estimation. Crump was good. The best. "Yeah, okay. What are we shooting? *Where* are we shooting?"

"Elmwood!" Anna piped up. Eric could tell she hoped it would rattle him, but Eric had practically grown up among the mossy headstones and monuments.

"The *cemetery*?" he asked, whipping back to Simon. "It's next door. What'd we have to drive all the way over here for?"

"To meet up with the group. C'mon!" Simon hauled on the van's sliding door and a wave of kids poured past Eric, hopping inside.

Five minutes after pulling in, Eric was tooling out of the lot with a hipster beside him at the wheel and Elvis drawling away behind him: "Rhythm is something you either have or don't have, but when you have it, you have it all over!"

The van lumbered down Central Avenue and circled past Annesdale Mansion on Snowden Circle. Eric wondered if this rattletrap could actually hold up for another half mile, but they arrived at the cemetery unscathed.

As the van pulled across the bridge and through the wrought-iron gates, Eric narrowed his eyes at a sign on the stone pillars. "They lock the place up at 4:30."

Ken cast him a side-glance. "You live next door. Don't tell me you've never been in here after dark."

Dwayne leaned in from the back. "Dude. Ken knows the gravedigger."

"Caretaker," Simon corrected.

"Just so long as you can get us all out," Eric warned. Ken braked, spun the wheel hard, and pulled into a spot by the chapel. As the kids piled out, Eric surveyed their lumpy backpacks with skepticism. "You've got costumes?"

Anna dragged out a bundle of clothes that looked like they'd just been rescued from a thrift store. She thrust them into Eric's arms. "Here. Rough these up. Rips, rub stuff in the dirt. You know, distress them."

Eric hesitated. He still wasn't sure how he'd gotten here, or how this counted as church—but Simon nudged him into action. "You better listen. She's producing this thing." Tugging out his pocketknife, Eric set to work on a long-sleeved gray shirt. "I don't know what 'this thing' is."

"Zombies!" Anna announced, tossing a full-scale makeup kit onto the grass beside a headstone.

Eric laughed. "You're going to be zombies. In a graveyard."

"Singing zombies," Michael clarified as he and Simon began grinding clothing into the dirt with their heels.

"Hey pompadour, you think real zombies can burp?" Dwayne asked as he screwed the lid off a two-liter Dr. Thunder and started chugging.

Instantly, the group pressed in with a rousing chorus of "Go, go, go, go . . . ."

Anna scrunched up her nose. "That is disgusting!" she declared. "You're gonna ruin the song."

Eric took a step back to escape the blast of Dwayne's impressive belch. "*What* song?"

Ken, who was busy selecting a camera lens, only smiled. "They wrote the lyrics. I claim no credit."

Anna began rubbing white makeup on Michael's face. "Yeah, if

anyone else can actually remember it all!" She took a deep breath and let loose with a surprisingly strong alto.

Oh, what a fright
I think my zits had taken over me
I felt dismembered like a lost zombie
That night I met you what a fright

As the other kids joined in, Eric was impressed anyone in this group had thought of using the *Four Seasons'* classic "Oh What a Night." And he was doubly glad they'd chosen a song with a strong beat—even if he did envy Gerry Polci for being safely in New Jersey instead of stuck in Elmwood Cemetery.

Oh, what a fright
You know I didn't even know your name
And then they made us play that awkward game
Middle school is such a fright

But I,
I got a funny feeling when you walked in with food
Oh my,
As I recall, it ended my bad mood

Eric tried not to laugh when Michael's zombie hit falsetto notes far above Elvis' range.

Oh, what a bite
Pizza always mesmerizes me
It was everything I dreamed it'd be
Pepperoni, what a bite

I felt the rush of a burning Dr. Thunder
Spinning my head around and taking away my hunger
Oh, what a bite

Oh, what a bite

Why'd it take so long to see the light
Now life's more than just my appetite
What a story, what a bite.

Oh what a bite! Doo dit doo dit dit doo dit doo dit dit

As the zombies started dancing, Anna cut them off. "Seriously, do any of you have a shred of rhythm?" She glanced over at Eric. "I mean, besides Eric . . . hey! You could sing with us."

"Whoa." Eric sprang up off the headstone he was using as a seat, and handed his newly distressed T-shirt to Simon. Anna's suggestion had crossed a line.

"But you're not actually drumming while we shoot," Simon pointed out.

Ken shoved a camera into Eric's hands. "I need him to shoot stills while I film you guys."

Eric breathed a sigh of relief. "Thanks, man," he muttered.

Within half an hour, the group of twelve-year-olds had transformed into surprisingly credible zombies. Eric scoped out the sprawling grounds of the cemetery with a new eye. "We could get some great shots right where Oak Avenue and East Crawford meet up, right there in the middle."

They raced the setting sun to grab the best lighting. "Magic hour," Ken called it. Chills crept up Eric's spine as his camera captured the zombies' long shadows, dancing across the stones of Memphians whose stories had ended a century ago. Dwayne appeared like a gargoyle, twisting and slithering over the looming Donahoe Vault. Even the absurd song, highlighted by Michael's Elvis zombie, was haunting when Eric considered how few breaths separated the stories above ground from those below it.

As the sun slipped behind the trees, Ken called a wrap and the group gathered for a quick debrief. Simon thumped his knuckles proudly against the battered monument where they'd finished and offered a mock bow to the group. "Allow me to present . . . Headless Sarah Somethington!" he announced.

Eric remembered seeing Sarah's statue before; time had taken not only her head, but one hand, and even part of her name. He tried to decipher the engraving in the dim light. "Atherington? Farmington?"

Ken slid his camera back into the bag. "Simon made me promise we'd include Sarah in the shoot." He pulled out an old black-and-white photograph and held it out to the group. "Take a look at this." Simon activated his phone flashlight, and the image danced to life: a young woman, hair piled high on her head, lace collar at her throat. Despite the formal pose, her eyes were live as coals. She seemed ready to stride off the page.

"Headless Sarah?" Eric questioned.

"Yup," Ken confirmed. "Found this in the archives and restored her."

"How'd she die?" Dwayne demanded.

Ken's face grew deadly serious. Eric was pretty sure he was the only one who'd seen the brief flash of mischief in Ken's eyes through the creeping dusk. The rest of the group sat down and leaned in as Ken began.

"Sarah lived in Memphis at the time of The Great Fever in 1878. People were falling ill by the hundreds. The thousands! Families fled the city, but Sarah stayed to nurse the sick and dying through seizures as their skin turned waxy yellow."

Every eye was fixed on Ken. But Eric caught a faint gesture

of Ken's hand—a signal. Smirking, Eric faded into the shadows, slipping around behind the kids.

"Sarah's touch seemed miraculous," Ken continued. "She'd lay her hand on the back of a victim's neck, like so. . . ." He touched two fingers to the nape of his own neck. "Within hours, the victim's fever would drop. Their skin would return to its normal color. It seemed certain they would recover! For two days at the height of the Fever, the whole city clamored for Sarah's touch." Ken paused, playing his audience like tightly tuned guitar strings. "But then . . . the Fever returned. Within 48 hours, those first few touched by Sarah were gripped with raging delirium. Fever blazed inside of them like fire until it scorched the very life out of them. They died. And so did every single Fever victim Sarah had touched."

Ken's gaze raked the group. Simon shivered. Michael's fingernails dug into his palms. "Did . . . did Sarah know what she was doing?" he croaked.

Ken's eye flickered briefly toward Eric. Carefully, Eric closed his right hand around a clammy water bottle as Ken continued. "No one knows. But one thing is certain. When all her victims lay dying . . . or as corpses, piled right here in this cemetery . . . Sarah stared in the mirror, devastated by what she saw in her own eyes."

Simon's eyes flashed briefly back. He spotted Eric, who shook his head in warning. Simon suppressed a grin.

Ken's voice reeled in the rest of the kids. "Then Sarah reached up . . . and back . . . and placed her cold fingers like so, right on her own neck . . ."

Eric laid his chilly fingers directly on the back of Michael's neck. Michael shrieked, octaves higher than Elvis,s he bolted away from Headless Sarah. For a moment, chaos reined as everyone scrambled away from the shadows—until they realized that Simon and Eric were nearly weeping with laugher.

Michael attempted to regain his dignity. "You have to put on a show for people in order to draw a crowd."

"Did that stuff about the Fever really happen?" Anna demanded, flouncing back toward Headless Sarah. She felt she hadn't represented her gender very well by fleeing along with the boys.

"Sure it did," Ken replied. "Though," he added, "I doubt Sarah caused any of it."

"So, you just made it up about her," Anna grumbled. "That's not fair."

"She had a chance to tell her own story when she was alive," Ken pointed out. "We all do—we just don't pay attention to it most of the time. That's why I've got you collecting things that represent your story in your boxes."

Simon's brow furrowed. "But what other people choose to do . . . that changes what happens to us. That's not fair either."

Ken shrugged. "I'm not sure fair is the point. Maybe your story is part of something bigger than your plans. Maybe it's more about what happens *in* you than what happens *to* you."

Eric shoved Ken's still camera into the bag. The evening had certainly been unlike anything he would have imagined when Simon conned him into it two days ago.

Ken slung the camera over his shoulder and motioned for the group to head out. "C'mon zombies. I've gotta get you back to the land of the living."

As the group trooped back toward the entrance, Simon fell into step beside Eric. "You would have made a good zombie, you

know." Eric shook his head as Dwayne scaled another vault to check what lay beyond the fence.

"Hey Simon," Dwayne called, pointing. "Isn't that your school over there?"

"Yeah." Simon was immediately guarded.

"Don't these guys go there, too?" Eric asked.

Simon shook his head. "Most of them go to Bellevue Middle."

Dwayne leapt down from over their heads. Eric was sure he'd break an ankle, but the kid landed intact. "Still having trouble with that jerkwad baseball player?" Dwayne asked Simon.

Simon stiffened. Eric could sense Ken falling back to listen, too. But Simon merely shook his head. "Everything's . . . fine." He picked up his pace, striding ahead of the other kids.

Ken turned to Eric. "You know what that's about?"

Eric shrugged. "No clue."

"He trusts you. Simon doesn't trust many people."

Eric jammed his hands into his pockets. Trust was an uncomfortable weight. It meant people counting on you. People expecting things of you. His band expected him to take them places. He should be practicing right now. He should be down on South Main or Beale Street, plying his firm handshake. . . .

"Really glad you came," Ken was saying. "Crump has a couple hours next Saturday to do the drum track. And if you're game, you could come play the drums for us next Sunday when we do our regular shtick at church. Without the zombies."

They were back at the van. Eric hesitated; his father's orders wouldn't change. Would it be so bad playing drums while he served out his sentence? "I'll think about it," he offered.

"If you're interested," Ken pressed, "you could actually co-lead this group with me. I travel some weekends, and it would be great to have someone else on tap. We don't get a lot of time with these kids, when it comes down to it."

Eric could feel Simon's eyes on him. But he shook his head as he opened the van door and watched the zombies pour in. "I'm a drummer, man. Let's just stick with that."

* * *

After Eric dropped him off, Simon sat on the front steps, beneath the glow of the porch light. He had told his mother he didn't mind being home alone while she worked the evening shift. But the house seemed chill and empty in her absence. He felt more connected with the world at large, here where he could see lights blinking on all along the street.

The front walk wasn't ideal for marbles, but he pulled them out anyway. The Joseph's Coat swirled in an infinite mix of color. He set it firmly on the pavement as he considered the week ahead, the story he was weaving so carefully to release Max from an equally complex web.

Simon was weary of working alone. He was running out of time, and he needed another mind, another pair of eyes, another set of hands. He glanced at the Rogers' shadows moving behind the curtains inside the warmly lit home next door. Eric had handled the zombies well. Simon had another drumming lesson Tuesday. He would decide about Eric then.

MONDAY

Surely the janitor knew how many students ate during the 11:47 lunch period. Surely he put out enough seats for everyone.

But everywhere Max looked, he met packed tables and faces deliberately turned away. Empty chairs were blocked with backpacks to indicate they were saved for some lucky kid who belonged there.

At a nearby table, three guys competed to see who could stuff the most tater tots in their mouth and still take a drink without spewing. It looked like one unfortunate, unibrowed kid was about to make himself sick, but Max would gladly have done the same if it could have earned him a place at the table.

The lunch tray was weighing heavily in his hands now. The trick was to keep moving as if you had a destination, so no one would see you standing alone and vulnerable. But Max was almost to the far side of the room. He couldn't stop, and he couldn't turn back. He needed a seat *now*. In desperation, he turned to a nearby table where the self-acknowledged geeks sat—but even they refused to meet his eyes.

This is all his fault, Max thought, even though the thought itself

"Everywhere Max looked, he met packed tables and faces deliberately turned away."

was worn out from overuse. Just this week he had come to the conclusion that he hated his father. There were two simple reasons. The first was obvious: Blake Matthews had uprooted his family from a comfortable life in the suburbs of Philadelphia and plopped them down in the sweaty, pulsing heart of Memphis. It was Blake's hometown, but to Max, it was Alcatraz, and there was no escape. Blake's vision was to re-energize the Memphis educational system, starting with this petri dish of a charter school. Max's vision was to survive the lunch hour without humiliation.

The second reason Max had determined to set himself against his father had haunted him since the day of his birth: his name. Max Matthews. Ma Ma. *Mama!* the other kids called him. In Philadelphia, the offhand nickname was friendly, if unflattering. But *Mama* had bled through Facebook from friends to friends-of-friends until here, in Memphis, it became poison. A curse that could only be wiped out by a great display of bravery, a clear act to show that he was neither a Mama's boy, nor under the thumb of his principal father.

The thought made him glance across the room toward Nick. And wonder of wonders, Nick met his eyes! The older boy even jerked his head toward the empty chair on his right. Giddy with his unexpected good fortune, Max hurried across the room and set down his tray with relief.

Nick barely acknowledged Max's presence as he continued joking with Brody and several eighth grade girls—but Max didn't mind. He firmly believed Nick was his ticket out of isolation. Loved and applauded by every teacher, Nick seemed to know each move he was going to make before he was required to make it. Life was a joke, and he knew all the punch lines. Just sitting at the same lunch table with Nick gave Max a glimmer of reflected glory.

Still, Max knew he was on shaky ground. He hadn't convinced Simon to join Nick's grand scheme. And just this morning, Nick had handed down a new ultimatum on an even riskier mission. But if Max could pull this off, it would surely prove his commitment beyond question.

He swallowed a bite of mashed potatoes and breathed deep. "Nick?"

Nick only took a long sip of berry blast juice drink, and Max was sure he'd been ignored. But then Nick turned with an air of mocking respect. "What?" he grinned.

Max choked on a gulp of lemonade: Nick's teeth were blue. Bright sky blue. At first, Max thought it must be the drink, but Brody was drinking the same thing—and his teeth weren't blue.

"Yes?" Nick asked with barely suppressed impatience.

Max could only stare, his mouth gaping wide.

Someone must have spiked Nick's drink. Someone was daring to challenge Nick's authority.

"There he is," growled Brody suddenly, and Max saw Simon crossing the lunchroom with a brown paper bag. Nick was up like a shot, and Max knew he'd missed his chance to say anything.

"Time to lock him down." Nick narrowed his eyes. Brody was on his feet, too. Max hesitated: Was he supposed to be part of this? Nick glanced back and jerked his head, iron in his glare. Max popped up instantly and followed. They cornered Simon before he made it to the trash bin by the kitchen.

"Hey guys." Simon was alert, but appeared amused by something. Max envied his ability to meet Nick's eyes with a level gaze. "Feeling a little blue, Nick?" Simon asked.

Max gasped, but Nick wasn't fazed. "Not at all. Now that you're accepting my generous offer of a place in our venture."

Simon shook his head. "I was referring to the state of your teeth."

"My teeth are fine, thanks."

"Um, actually . . . ," Max stuttered. Nick caught the panic in Max's eyes and calmly glanced at his reflection in the glass covering next month's lunch menu. The cool fled as Nick caught sight of his bright blue teeth. "What the—" But he swallowed the outburst as he glimpsed Mr. Matthews on the far side of the room. Instead, he continued through pinched lips. "All right, Mr. Smith. You *will* help us access the database."

Simon didn't break the gaze. "The school's network is locked down from outside access. You'd have to set up from an administrative computer. "

"We got it covered," Brody snapped.

"And you'd have to have an SQL injection to create a new user—one with the access you need."

"Very good," Nick taunted, lips curled to hide his teeth. "That's your job."

"What if I don't do it?" Simon's eyes strayed to Max, who quickly focused on the ketchup-splattered floor at his feet.

"I think you know it won't be . . . pleasant." Nick smirked. "Go through with it and we cut you into the profits."

Simon nodded, slowly. Nick's eyes narrowed, but Brody jabbed him with an elbow as Mr. Matthews worked his way through the lunch tables toward them. Max swallowed hard. Nick arranged his features into a friendly smile as he hissed at Simon, "You've got until the end of the day tomorrow to get us the code."

"All right," Simon flashed back. "Meet me in the cemetery. Look for Headless Sarah near the big oak."

Nick and Brody exchanged a quizzical glance, but there was no time to clarify. In moments, Mr. Matthews was beside them. "Hello, boys," he said, smiling broadly at Nick.

"Hello, sir," Nick replied evenly. Max could tell it pained Nick not to return the smile, but he managed to pull it off smoothly, even without revealing his teeth. "Thanks for getting grilled chicken back on the menu," he said. "Great fuel for when I'm out there on the ball field. Really appreciate it."

"You're welcome, Mr. Darby," the principal replied, before turning to Simon. "Mr. Smith, I'd like to see you in my office in . . ." he checked his watch. "Let's make it five minutes, all right?" He smiled again at the boys, and strode out of the room.

Max felt a sudden tightness in his throat. There were moments at school when his dad didn't even seem to notice him. Not that Max wanted him to.

"Keep your mouth zipped, Smith," Nick was commanding Simon. He grabbed his own lunch tray. "C'mon, Mama," he ordered Max, who winced. Nick had not used the nickname before. It twisted deep.

Miserably, Max followed Nick to deposit their lunch trays and trailed him out into the hall. Several kids whispered and craned to catch a glimpse of Nick's mouth. He clamped his lips shut. "Why didn't you tell me about my teeth, Mama?" he hissed. Max shook his head, but Nick was already moving on. "Whoever pulled this stunt will pay," he commented with a casual ease that Max knew spelled danger. "Now get the right key, okay? We need a master. One of the greens."

"I *know* which key," Max mumbled.

"Don't foul this—" Nick broke off. They'd reached his locker. Plastered on the front of the door was a glossy photograph of AMS Reaper's Facebook page. A pair of fiery red eyes mocked from

beneath a dark hood in the profile picture.

Max had seen those eyes glowering on his own Facebook page beside a post from AMS Reaper—a terrible photo of an unknown fat kid completely jammed inside a school locker. Max had deleted the photo immediately, but he hadn't been able to erase the image from his mind, or the haunting whisper that Nick might have something to do with it.

"Ha!" Nick laughed. "Whoever they are, they can't prove anything." He ripped down the photo and yanked open his locker. Inside, on the shelf, sat an empty bottle of blue food coloring. The shade matched Nick's teeth to perfection.

Max's eyes widened. He had never seen someone get the best of Nick. It was unsettling, to see his idol made ridiculous—if only for a moment.

Nick's gaze shifted from the dye to the glossy photo. Then his eyes locked on Max. "What are you staring at?" he barked. "It's probably that Merona kid with his camera. I'll deal with him after Friday."

Max had watched James Merona in Biology class. James was too jittery to dissect a frog. Max wouldn't have guessed he had the guts to take on Nick, but appearances could be deceiving.

"What are you waiting for?" Nick snapped, blue teeth flashing. "Go do your job. And stay out of my way 'til the cemetery."

Max turned and fled.

* * *

Simon trotted down the hallway, warmed by a small glow of satisfaction. For the first time ever, he had seen Nick flinch. And he had bought himself another day. Only the memory of Max's strained

face gave him pause.

Ahead, Simon could see Mr. Matthews approaching the door to his office. Simon studied the principal's quick stride and the way he ran his hand back to front across his hair, as if the pressure might clear his mind. As Mr. Matthews gripped his office doorknob and felt it give, Simon could see a small frown on the principal's face. He must have meant to lock it.

By the time Simon caught up, Mr. Matthews was already inside. Simon rapped briefly on the half-open door and entered to the principal's "Come in!"

Simon had been in Mr. Matthews' office before. Unlike the rest of the administrative offices, it stood by itself in an odd angle of the renovated building. And unlike the other offices, this one was designed to make students feel at ease. On one side of the desk, which faced the door, sat an intricate metal marble roller, twisting and turning at fascinating angles. Mr. Matthews' magnificent marble collection filled jars and trays on a table beside it. A high-backed armchair with fraying corduroy and a series of tall bookshelves took up the other side of the office.

Mr. Matthews' back was turned as he searched for a file on the shelf behind his desk. "Take a seat, Simon," he said.

Usually, the marbles drew Simon's immediate attention. But today, he spotted a flash of movement behind the armchair. Fascinated, he took a step to the side, craning his neck . . .

And locked eyes with Max, crouched down low, out of his father's line of sight.

Max's expression was a mix of defiance and pleading. He jabbed a finger toward a bookshelf, several steps closer to Mr. Matthews' desk. Simon could see one of the distinctive copper school keys lying there. The engraved green "M" marked it as a master key—an

"Usually, the marbles drew Simon's immediate attention. But today . . ."

extra apparently, since Mr. Matthews' key ring sat on his desk.

"Simon?" Mr. Matthews' voice snapped Simon to attention.

"Uh, sorry, sir." Simon quickly dropped into a guest chair that allowed him to see both Max and the principal. He immediately wished he hadn't, because Max's gestures were becoming frantic.

"I know you've got to get to fourth period, so I won't keep you," Mr. Matthews explained. "Your Computer Apps teacher says you're way ahead of the curve when it comes to navigating new applications. We're forming a student team to advise us on some new software for next year, and I'd like you to be a part of it."

"I . . . that would be great, sir," Simon stumbled.

"Once the auditors re-certify the school this week, we'll have an extra boost of technology funding for next year. We think student input will be very valuable."

"It's a great idea," Simon agreed, his mind racing. At any other time, he would be over the moon to receive such an offer from Mr. Matthews. But right now his brain felt like loose marbles. A massive cheating scandal could torpedo the school's chances for re-certification if it came to light. It would be easy, so easy, to turn Max in and be done with it. But that would lead to complications that Simon's brain didn't have time to unravel in split seconds.

And at this moment, Max had chosen to trust Simon. It was something Simon couldn't throw away, frustrated as he was.

"Thank you, Simon," Mr. Matthews nodded. "I've got some information about the advisory team I'd like you to take with you . . . if I can find it . . ." He gave up on the shelf behind his desk and turned toward the bookshelves. In two steps, he would spy Max.

Simon read the panic in Max's eyes. Bolting to his feet, he

stepped forward, blocking Mr. Matthews' path. "I can just come back later, when you've found it." He could sense movement behind him. The master key burned at the edge of his vision; Max needed an opening.

Simon waved toward the elaborate marble roller. "Did you build that yourself?" He felt rather than heard Max move, and waved a frantic hand behind his back to stop the younger boy.

"No." Mr. Matthews shook his head. "But I designed it."

"Could you show me?" Simon asked.

To his relief, Mr. Matthews circled around the desk, his back now turned toward the armchair. As the principal pointed out the individual slides and trays, the pulleys and wheels, Simon stole a quick glance back at Max—who was still frozen.

"Go!" he mouthed. Max sprang into action, launching forward and swiping the key. But as he prepared to beeline for the door, Mr. Matthews turned toward Simon again. Max dove back behind the armchair.

"I find that kids are always fascinated by marbles. . . well, not just kids," Mr. Matthews admitted.

Simon tried hard not to glance behind. "So you and Max must play a lot, right?" he asked.

Mr. Matthews shook his head, and Simon realized he'd hit a nerve. "No. No, Max has never really gotten into marbles."

"That's funny," Simon commented, tracing one of the spiraling slides with his finger. "Because Max seems to be the kind of guy who likes to go in circles." He hoped the verbal dart hit home as he slid around to the other side of the marble roller, trying to draw Mr. Matthews' focus.

As he brushed by the marble table, he saw it, just as he remembered from last time: a jar filled with nothing but rare antique Swirls.

It wasn't part of the plan, but Simon couldn't help himself. "That's a pretty cool Latticinio," he commented pointing to one of the Swirls in the jar. "You've really got an awesome collection." He didn't need to look at Mr. Matthews' face to note the surprise.

"You play?" Mr. Matthews asked. "You're a collector?"

"Yeah," Simon told him as his hand strayed to the marble in his own pocket. "I mean . . . kinda."

The brief silence that followed reminded Simon this diversion was costing Max, big time. The bell for fourth period shrilled, releasing Simon like a spring. "Oh, hey!" he babbled. "I've gotta try this before I leave!"

Without waiting for Mr. Matthews' permission, he grabbed a jar of mint condition Aggies. Stretching, he upended them all into the feeder at the top of the marble roller.

"Wait! Not so many!" Mr. Matthews cried, but the clatter and racket of two dozen descending marbles drowned out his voice, and he and Simon both crouched to collect the rain of marbles jumping their chutes.

Simon cast a quick glance over his shoulder. Through the hail of marbles, he saw Max scurry from behind the chair, careen across the room, and slide out the door.

The staccato shots of marbles hitting brick and concrete finally died out. Breathless, Simon handed the marbles he'd corralled back to a stunned Mr. Matthews. "I'm really sorry!" he offered. "It's such a cool roller."

"I think you need to get to class." Mr. Matthews frowned, but Simon was pretty sure he was hiding a smile.

"Yes, thank you, I'll come back for the information!" Simon said, and darted out of the room. He glanced both ways down the hall, hoping to catch sight of Max. But the halls had cleared. Max was gone.

TUESDAY

Nick's face was yellow. Ripe banana yellow.

Max knew his own face was red from pounding down the hall, trying to catch Nick after gym. He couldn't afford to make the same mistake twice. This time, Max would be quick and decisive and tell Nick before anyone else could. He would speak as an equal. He opened his mouth—but instead blurted out, "I've got the key!"

"Shut up!" Nick hissed, and Max noticed Mrs. Kingsbury, the school secretary, pass by just a sort distance away. Trembling, Max closed his fist around the key and tried to hand it to Nick, but the older boy halted him with a steely glare. "Not on school grounds, Mama. You're meeting us in the cemetery, remember? After the final bell."

Max jammed the key back in his pocket and shifted on unsteady feet. "Uh, Nick?" he fumbled. "Did you know your face—"

But before he could choke out the rest of the sentence, Simon sauntered past on the way to his locker. "Hey, Nicholas," he smirked. "Yellow's not really your color."

Nick offered Simon a cold smile. "Aren't you the fashion critic?" But as soon as Simon was past, Nick rolled his eyes. "I'm not even wearing yellow."

Numb, Max stared after Simon. "It's your face," he offered apologetically.

Nick stopped cold. "What about my face, Mama?" he snapped. But even as he said it, he rubbed his fingers across his forehead and stared at them: tinged with yellow.

Max tried to ignore the ripe scent of gym socks and decaying ham sandwich that wafted from Nick's half-open gym bag. He couldn't bring himself to speak. Instead, he watched as Nick reconstructed a plausible series of events to explain the color of his face.

"Sunscreen. I always wear sunscreen," Nick concluded. "Merona's got gym with me. He could have messed with it. Now, quit staring and get out of here!"

Nick stalked away, leaving Max with a sinking feeling in his stomach. But he had to know. Careful to stay unnoticed amid the flood of students in the hallway, Max followed.

Sure enough, a large photograph covered the front of Nick's locker. This one showed a Facebook login page. The user name read: "AMS Reaper." The password was filled in, too—revealed by a string of dots. A pointer hand hovered over the "login" button, ready to click. It was as if the photographer had watched the Reaper log in . . . or somehow discovered the Reaper's account information. Max's head spun as he tried to understand the message.

But Max only had a moment to think before he noticed his father walking down the hall. Beside Mr. Matthews trotted a rumpled little man with sharp eyes—one of the auditors evaluating the school for charter renewal, Mr. Garlic, or something like that.

With no time to remove the incriminating photograph, Nick plastered his back against the locker door. This gave Mr. Matthews a direct view of Nick's bright yellow face.

"Mr. Darby!" he exclaimed. "Is everything all right?"

Nick smiled, and Max had to give him credit for polish under pressure. "Just showing my school spirit," Nick explained. "Sporting the old gold and blue."

Mr. Matthews smiled at the auditor. "Amazing how these kids have built up such a school identity in just two years, isn't it?" Then to Nick he added, "Carry on!" and continued down the hall with the auditor.

Max watched with a hawk's eye as Nick ripped down the photo and opened his locker door. A bottle sat on the shelf inside.

Yellow dye.

* * *

Simon checked his phone as he adjusted his backpack and hurried across the train tracks south of the school building. 3:26. He slipped through the hole in the fence and stopped to catch his breath once he reached the paved lane. Then he jogged along the perimeter, cutting across the grass when he spied Headless Sarah.

He was in luck. Max was already there, alone, gazing uneasily at Sarah's lichen-green dress. Simon was tempted to place his hand on the back of Max's neck, but refrained. Instead, he called out, "Max!"

Max jumped and swiveled. "Don't *do* that!"

"It's just Headless Sarah," Simon said wryly. "She did all her

damage 130 years ago."

"Fine for you. I didn't grow up running around this . . . place."
Max crossed his arms, as if to keep all the thousands of monuments
at bay.

Simon studied Max again. He didn't look anything like Mr.
Matthews: stocky, pale, and dark-haired. "Look Max, you don't
need Nick and Brody."

Max glared at a carved angel across the path. "You have no
idea what I need."

Simon rubbed his head in frustration. If only Max would swallow
his pride and make a quick exit from the whole scheme. "They're
going to pin this whole thing on you," he pointed out. "You can
back out while there's still time left."

"It's no big deal. Just stupid grades."

Simon wanted to shake Max, but he forced himself to stay calm.
"Once Nick's in the database, he can get to anything he wants.
Social Security numbers. Teachers' addresses. Don't think your dad
can just get you out of it!"

Simon knew immediately those last words had been a mistake.
Max stiffened. "I can take care of myself!"

"And how's that working out for you?"

"I know what I'm doing," Max fumbled in his pocket and
produced the master key. He held it high, where it glinted in the
sunlight. "They can't do this without *me*. I've got control of the
whole thing, right here—"

Nick swooped in, popping the key out of Max's hand. He stood
at ease, adjusting his signature messenger cap. It irked Nick that

hats were not allowed in school; he always kept the cap in his bag, ready to rock it once he left the building.

"Well, well. Looks like Mama's not a total loss," he drawled.

Instinctively, Simon stepped forward to place himself in front of Max. Nick narrowed his eyes. But before he could take action, Brody piped up, "Can we get out of here already?"

Simon raised an eyebrow as he noted Brody trying to watch his own back from every angle. "What?" Simon asked, innocent. "Afraid of Headless Sarah's ghost?"

"You're the one who should be afraid," Brody threatened.

"Right." Simon nodded toward Sarah, savoring the moment. "Her ghost is pretty harmless. It's the Fever I'd worry about."

"Fever?" croaked Brody.

"Yeah, she died during the Yellow Fever epidemic. They say the virus can hibernate for years."

Brody was sweating now, skin clammy. Nick cuffed him upside the head. "The virus couldn't last for a century, lame brain."

Nick took a step closer to Simon. The older boy had gotten his growth spurt early; he towered over Simon and Max. "Cut the crap," he demanded, flashing the key. "We've got access to an admin terminal now. Where's the code for the SQL injection?"

Simon stood his ground. "I told you. It takes time."

"How do I know you're not playing me?"

"You've got my word." Simon couldn't resist adding, "Which is worth a lot more than yours."

"See, Smith. That's where you're wrong. When I promise to cause pain, I follow through." He rapped his fist against Sarah and then leaned up against the cold stone. "I thought Mama explained this to you. I have friends at Bartlett who can get anything I ask for. One false move and you'll both find yourselves *in possession*—with the admin on your tails. And then you're suspended. Out." Nick tilted his head. "Right, Brody?"

"Right. Yeah." Brody closed in on Max and Simon from behind, but Simon sidestepped out of his path. He had no doubt that Nick could get his hands on any illegal substance he wanted.

"Wow," Simon began. "You've sure given me something to think about. That ought to make coding move a lot faster." Nick nodded to Brody, who grabbed Simon's arm. "Hey! Back off." Simon flailed, trying to slip from Brody's grasp. He knew he could match Nick and Brody wit for wit, but an actual fight was another matter. He twisted once more, tearing free, but smashing his cheek against the stub of Headless Sarah's arm. The blow numbed half his face. He knew it would sting badly in a few minutes.

"Max." Nick commanded coolly, and Simon could see the next few minutes unfolding in his mind's eye: Nick would force Max to fight Simon, probably while Brody held him down. Simon could take pain, but he wasn't sure that Max could handle giving it.

"Just stop!" Simon cried out.

"Had enough?" Nick smirked.

"I'll do it, okay? I'll write out the code for you."

"Tomorrow," Nick ordered.

"No." Simon stood his ground. "Friday evening, during the fundraiser. You said yourself, you don't *need* to be in before then."

"Simon stood his ground."

He could see Nick's surprised skepticism, but plunged ahead. "That master key is only for interior doors. On Friday, the school building will be open, but everyone will be outside, distracted. It's the perfect time."

Nick considered for a long moment. Simon could feel Brody's glower, Max's barely veiled panic. Then Nick flicked a dead cicada off Sarah's arm and nodded.

"You're on."

★ ★ ★

Simon waited until he reached Willam Spandow's headstone to stop for a breath. His heart was pounding loudly in his ears as he dropped down onto the turf.

He pulled out the Joseph's Coat, working it back and forth in his palm as his eyes flickered across William's memorial:

Killed in chemical laboratory of
Columbia University
by an explosion
due to the carelessness of others

Bitterness still oozed fresh from the grave, nearly a century later. There was danger in trusting other people. But Simon knew he could no longer work alone.

★ ★ ★

Eric braked hard as he pulled into the driveway. He could feel the pads grinding on metal, but so far, the El Camino had always managed to stop. He didn't have the money for a brake job. And if he told his father, Marcus would prod him to buy some environmentally friendly tin can on wheels with a loan larger than the car itself. Eric didn't like to owe anyone. Especially not his parents.

As he hopped out of the car, he spotted Simon plowing up the sidewalk. "Hey!" Eric called. "You got a lesson."

Simon paused in front of his own house and glanced up at Eric. "Gotta get my sticks."

Eric stared. The left side of Simon's face was an angry, swollen red. "What's with your face?" Eric asked. "Last week you skip, now this?"

"It was Headless Sarah." Simon smiled faintly. "She's got a mean left."

"She doesn't *have* a right." Eric crossed his arms. Waiting.

"Just let me get my drumsticks, okay?" Simon disappeared up the walk and into his house as Eric headed for the shed in his backyard. Before Eric even reached the shed, Simon popped out of his own back door and launched himself over the rail fence. He proudly gripped a pair of well-taped drumsticks. Eric suppressed a grin as he unlocked the shed door. Simon's sticks didn't get the kind of use that needed tape. Eric had never thought of himself as the kind of guy someone would want to copy.

Simon followed Eric into the shed. It was like stepping into a different world. The homemade sound panels Eric had hung last summer to appease the neighbors did more than deaden noise. They made things feel safe. Separate. As if inside this room, the rest of the world didn't exist.

Drums filled the small space from wall to wall. Simon guessed the bottle-green custom acrylic set had cost Eric a whole summer's salary at the Drum Shop. Simon wasn't allowed to touch it, but he could try anything else. Every set Eric had ever used was stored in the shed. Then there were the brake drums, trashcan lids, and other oddities Eric had rescued from garage sales or junkyards, each item

chosen for its unique sound.

Simon took his seat at an older drum set and tried not to think about how little he'd practiced on his drum pads that week. "You want me to start with paradiddles?"

But Eric hadn't moved out of the doorway. "No. I want you to start by telling me what the hell happened to you."

Eric wasn't sure why it was so important to know what Simon had been up to. After all, he'd been assigning rudiments to Simon the whole year with no need to pry. But the kid didn't have a dad or older brother to look out for him, and he was clearly on the wrong end of someone's temper.

Simon shifted on his seat. Telling part of the story would mean telling the whole story—so he tried to shrug it off. "I told you," he repeated, "Sarah's up to her tricks."

Eric stalked closer to stand over him. "Seriously."

Simon's sweaty palm was making the drumsticks slick. He wiped his hand on his jeans and looked Eric squarely in the face. "All right," he offered. "I'll tell you what happened." Then he added, daring. "*If* you come and play drums for us on Sunday."

Eric raised his eyebrows as he planted himself on the seat at the custom drum set. "What's with you and the bribery?" He accented it with a triple stroke roll. "You tell me or you don't get a lesson."

"You wouldn't do that," Simon countered. "Mom's paid up through the end of the month."

"Watch me!" Eric spatted the drumheads.

Diggada cha chiggata dat digga doom gat!

Eric knew he was showing off, but he wasn't going to be roped into anything. Simon took the display as a challenge and laid down a rhythm himself.

Chiggada chiggada gok gok chiggada gok!

The kid wasn't half bad, Eric had to admit. But he couldn't let it go. Instead, he launched into a new drum break he'd been building. Simon threw in a few beats, but Eric wore him out in moments, sticks flying fast and furious, cymbals swinging, drumheads exploding into sound. The shed around them vibrated. The pulsing beats were set to blast the roof off.

BAM!

The snare head burst, and one of Eric's sticks almost flew out of his hand.

"*Da—*" Eric choked it down and glared at Simon. The younger boy stared back, unfazed.

"It's okay. I've heard worse," Simon deadpanned.

Eric frowned. The kid needed some serious schooling. Eric opened his mouth to chew Simon out. But instead, he felt his grimace cracking. And then he laughed. He couldn't help it; Simon looked as smug as if he'd engineered the whole thing himself.

"I should charge you for this head," Eric claimed.

"You're the one who gets a discount at the Drum Shop," Simon pointed out.

"I'll come and drum at your churchy thing on Sunday, okay? Whether or not you cut loose about your shady activities."

"You're one to talk," Simon scoffed. "What about that concert

on top of Annesdale?"

"You're jealous? You want a police record, too?"

It was uncomfortable reminder of Nick's threat. Simon studied Eric for another long moment. He, Simon, would have to take the plunge. "What I really want," he announced, "is barbecue."

"You're outta luck, man. I don't cook."

"My mom's working tonight. You could take me to Tops."

"We'll see." Eric shook his head. "*After* your lesson."

* * *

As he wiped barbecue sauce off his chin, Eric considered how easily Lisa had let him off the hook on family dinner when she heard what he was planning.

She had cast him a surprised glance as she pulled a pan of Brussels sprouts from the oven. "I'm glad you're looking after Simon. Diane mentioned she has to cover some extra evening shifts this week, and I know she hates to leave him."

Eric had shrugged. "He can take care of himself. I just hate Brussels sprouts, that's all."

Still, it was the first time in months his mother had seemed pleased with his choices. In a rush of goodwill, he had even volunteered to go with her and Marcus to the neighborhood fundraiser at Annesdale Middle on Friday.

Annesdale Middle—Simon's school, he realized as Simon put away his third barbecue sandwich without slowing down. Eric shook his head and tapped their stained table. "This place is a dump."

"So?" Simon grinned between mouthfuls. "Good food."

"You on your own a lot? For meals." Eric hoped it sounded casual. He should just drop this.

"Not really. Mom just has to work extra this week 'cause someone at the hospital quit."

Eric surveyed Simon's face. The red patch was fading to sick shades of purple and green. "That why she doesn't know what's up with you?"

"Nah. Mom knows pretty much everything." Simon chewed his mouthful of barbecue for so long that Eric thought he'd shut the kid down. Finally, Simon swallowed and took a deep breath. "Except . . . there's this . . . situation," he began.

"At that fancy charter school of yours?"

"It's just a school." Simon took a long drink of lemonade. And then he plunged in. He laid out the whole story for Eric, from lunchroom threats and Max's thievery to the run-in with Headless Sarah's snapped-off wrist. He kept back only one thing. One secret.

"So, wait." Eric's head was spinning. "I missed the part about why you don't just turn these jerks in. To your principal, that Mr. Marky . . . Mathison. . .?"

"Matthews."

"Right. Him."

Simon sighed and stirred around the last shreds of slaw with his fork. "It'll be better to catch Nick in the act. The teachers love him. They'll believe anything he says unless there's evidence. A *lot* of evidence."

"What about that Max kid?"

"I can't let Max take the fall! I've got to get him out first. He needs to see the truth about Nick and Brody on his own."

"Why do you care? He sounds like a wuss."

"He's had a rough year. I've just got to, okay?" Simon barreled on before Eric could protest. "I only need 'til Friday."

"What happens then?"

Simon grinned. "That's where you come in!"

"Whoa. Hold it. Back up!" It was one thing to hear Simon out. It was another thing to get stuck in this mess himself.

"Well, I can't be everywhere at once. But if you help, we can get Max out *and* catch Nick and Brody in action." Simon decided full disclosure was the best policy, so he added, "Okay, we might need Dwayne and Michael and Anna, too."

"I fail to see how an Elvis impersonator is going to solve this," Eric retorted.

"Just trust me," Simon told him, grabbing a plastic Tops pen. "I've got it all worked out."

Eric knew he should shut the whole thing down, but Simon's plan was pretty impressive, as he diagrammed it across three napkins and a Styrofoam cup. Simon even highlighted the key points of attack with barbecue sauce. And somehow, before dropping Simon off after dinner, Eric found himself agreeing to go through with it.

"Three days," he warned Simon. "This doesn't work out by then and you . . . *we* are going to . . . Mr. Matthews. Or your group leader, that Ken guy."

Eric watched the front door swing shut behind Simon, but he didn't go home. Instead, he coasted through the neighborhood, cutting up Snowden Avenue past Annesdale Mansion. The arched windows and columns were barely visible through the trees. He thought about calling Israel to pull off another late night concert on the roof, but he didn't want to push his luck. Especially not with the concert scheduled for tomorrow night.

Eric found himself strangely pleased that Simon had chosen to trust him. Still, a nagging voice in the back of his mind whispered he was going in too deep, too fast. Time was running out. For a moment he thought about calling Ken after all, but he hadn't gotten Ken's number. He couldn't even remember Ken's last name.

No, he would let this play out. For now.

Arriving home, he pulled into the driveway and rolled past the house into the backyard. Marcus hated what it did to the grass, but Eric had a lot of equipment to load up for tomorrow.

And a snare head to replace, he thought wryly as he flipped on the shed light.

"The crowd at the riverfront was the largest Eric had ever drawn."

WEDNESDAY

The crowd at the riverfront was the largest Eric had ever drawn. A few hundred people packed the lawn near the stage as park lamps cast bright reflections on the dark water beyond. But it was nothing compared to what the place would be like in a couple of days. So many music lovers would pack into Tom Lee Park for Memphis in May you wouldn't be able to see the grass.

Eric's band, Bright Midnight, was a warm-up act, a chance to test out one of the stages and the sound system. In a few years, though, Eric planned to be one of the big names, playing alongside groups like Dave Matthews Band and Foo Fighters.

As his wrists worked double-time on the drums and his voice carried the music, Eric's eyes drifted to the statue of Tom Lee—the park's namesake. When a steamer had capsized almost a century ago, Tom had hauled 32 people out of the river . . . even though he couldn't swim.

This weekend, Eric figured, the music would try to do the same thing: save drowning people. That's why all of Memphis turned out along the riverbank. It was why people listened. If there was a God, He was in the music. At least that's where Eric felt the most alive.

Eric's eyes raked across the faces in the audience. He was surprised to spy a group of kids in the front. He blinked, looked again, and nearly missed a beat: Simon, Michael, Dwayne, and Anna grinned, waving wildly. Eric usually maintained a cool gaze on stage, but he couldn't help cracking a tiny smile. They were crazy showing up here like this, but at least they weren't sporting their zombie makeup. He recovered his poker face, but finished the set with an extra burst of energy.

Afterward, the kids swarmed him onstage. Israel shook his head and the other guys smirked, but Eric didn't care.

"Don't disrespect our next-gen fan base," Eric warned.

Michael stuck out his hand to Israel and offered his best Elvis. "I'd just like to be treated like a regular customer," he drawled.

Israel shook his head, but took Michael's hand anyway. "The King lives!" he mocked, good-natured.

Simon examined Eric's drum set. "You replaced the head."

Eric raised an eyebrow. "What, you thought I'd play with a busted head? How'd you get down here, anyway?"

"The trolley!" Dwayne announced. "It was pretty awesome."

Anna rolled her eyes. "I've been on the trolley like a million times."

"Don't you have curfews and stuff?" Eric razzed.

They did. In fact, Anna's mom was down the grass, waving for them to hurry up. Simon shot Eric a significant glance as the kids left. Clearly, the game was still on. Eric wasn't sure if he was glad or panicked.

As Eric went back to break down his drum kit, he discovered the kids hadn't been his only guests.

"Good show." Eric looked up to see Ken, camera slung around his neck.

"Thanks." Nodding at the camera, Eric added, "You looking for B-roll for that zombie flick?"

Ken laughed. "I had a shoot earlier. But I thought I'd come check out our celebrity drummer in action."

"Right." Eric smiled. Then struck by a sudden thought, he asked, "Hey! You didn't get any shots of the band, did you?" Just this week, the members of Bright Midnight had been griping about their less-than-inspiring promo photos.

"I got a few," Ken admitted. "Not sure they're any good, but you're welcome to take a look." He held out the camera. As Eric scrolled through the images, he inhaled sharply, surprised. Somehow, Ken had captured Eric's passion in a single flash. His hands and wrists, the drumsticks, were at the heart of one image. Stage lights spilled across his face, which glowed strong and alive.

"Nice," Eric acknowledged. "Can I get a copy of these?" he asked, turning back to scroll through some more.

"Yeah. I could probably dump the images on a flash drive," Ken offered. "My studio's just a block down on South Main if you want them now. Or I can get them to Simon next week."

Eric didn't hesitate. He wanted these photos. And there was the thing with Simon, too; he needed advice. Buckling down the last of his drum kit, he nodded. "Why not? Let me run this out to the Camino, and we'll go now."

* * *

Dozens of framed photographs covered the walls of Ken's studio—but each one had breathing room. Eric spotted prints of music greats and pictures from downtown Memphis parks. But most of the photos showed people in various locations around the city. The images seemed natural rather than posed. There was something almost magical about the way Ken could catch someone at just the right moment.

"Hey, there's Headless Sarah!" Eric stopped in front of the restored photograph Ken had shown them Sunday, now enlarged and framed. "I mean . . . Sarah with her head."

"That's a good one," Ken agreed. "I went looking for her because I knew Simon liked the marker, but I love how she's so direct. In those early photos, most people look like the camera's about to spray bullets. She doesn't show an ounce of fear."

Eric moved on to the black-and-white photograph of a wispy-haired little girl sitting beneath the rotunda of a crumbling building. She was drawing swirls in the dust. "Is that the abandoned police station on Adams?" he asked. "It looks like a dump on the outside, but this is really cool."

Ken nodded. "It has a lot to do with focus and lighting. Photographers learn how to lead people to see what we want them to see. The goal is to focus on one thing—to freeze that one moment in time that tells a story." He pointed to the next image. "Check this one out. What do you see?"

Eric studied the photograph: a border collie perched on the seat of a horse-drawn carriage. A street lamp cast its light directly on the dog as it sat upright and alert, gazing up at its master, the paunchy driver.

"I've seen that guy!" Eric exclaimed. "He's a real Oscar the Grouch. Always crabbing at people to get out of his way."

"The goal is to focus on one thing—to freeze that one moment in time that tells a story."

"But look at his dog," Ken said.

"Border collie," Eric commented. "You never see them sit still like that."

"It's interesting to me how the dog's completely focused on the driver," Ken pointed out. "It's my tribute to the idea of unconditional love. It reminds me there's another side to people that we don't always see. Imagine if you could see the driver through his dog's eyes."

"Yeah, well. Dogs are a lot nicer than people." Eric pointed to a bare spot further down the wall. "What goes here?"

"Had a great shot of a couple kids crossing the I-55 bridge there, but someone bought it today." Ken had removed the memory card from his camera and was pulling the images onto a MacBook. He paused as the photo of Eric flashed onto the screen. "Actually, I might use this one. If you don't mind."

"Do I get royalties?" Eric wisecracked.

"You'll be hanging three feet from B.B. King." Ken nodded toward an image further down the wall. "I shot that when he recorded his live CD in Memphis."

"Fair enough," Eric agreed. He looked back at the photo on Ken's computer screen—he'd never seen someone capture a clearer image of his passion for music. "Wish my dad could see that," he noted, unsure why he said it, or where the bitterness came from. "They want me going to school for some lame business degree," he explained.

Ken nodded slowly. "I guess things always look different from the other side of the lens. You ever try to flip it?" Ken spun his camera 180 degrees on the counter.

Eric gripped the drumsticks in his back pocket. "I don't know. I guess . . . they don't want me wasting time. We just don't quite see eye to eye on what that means."

"So, you don't want to waste your time on anything other than your music career?" Ken glanced up at Eric for confirmation.

Eric shrugged. "Aren't we supposed to do what we love doing?"

"Yeah, I get that. I can't imagine my life without photography," Ken agreed. Then smirking, he added, "It must suck having parents who want to manipulate your life by getting you to finish your education."

"Right. I get it. They care about me," Eric conceded. "I'm just not sure they'll ever understand about music. What I want is me, main stage at the Beale Street Music Festival, touring the country, giving people the kind of music that moves their souls."

"I like that part of your story." Ken handed Eric a flash drive with the night's images. "Just remember your story is bigger than your music. Don't miss the rest of the story that's happening around you. Your family has a story. Other people, too."

Eric wasn't sure whether to be relieved or irritated. "You're talking about Simon," he guessed.

"You're good at reading people, you know?" Ken smiled. "I can tell something's up with Simon, but that kid's a stone wall if he doesn't want to tell you. Has he talked to you?"

"Sort of. Yeah." Now that Ken asked, Eric wasn't sure he knew where to start. He wanted to tell the whole complicated story. But would Simon consider it a broken confidence?

"Anything to worry about? With Simon?"

"Um, maybe," he finally replied. "But I think I've got it for now. Things should be clearer by Friday." Eric paused. There was no easy way to explain. "I'll let you know."

"Well, you can catch me anytime if you need help." Ken handed over his card. Eric shoved it in his pocket with the flash drive as he caught sight of the clock. He still had another three weeks to haul himself out of bed early for high school. "Thanks, man," he said, and started for the door. "I gotta go."

As he reached the door, Ken called out, "Simon says you're going to play drums for us."

Eric laughed. "Yeah, he talked me into it. Plus that zombie drum track."

"What I said about leading Simon's group with me, it still stands. He already trusts you, so you're way ahead of the game."

The door was already halfway open, the air cool on Eric's face. He hesitated. "I told you. I'm just a drummer."

He didn't look back through the glass as the door closed behind him. He didn't want to see disappointment in Ken's face.

THURSDAY

Diane spun into the kitchen like a small tornado, keys in hand. She checked the back of the door. No lab coat. She darted into the hall. It wasn't on the coat rack.

"You washed them!" Simon called. Diane whirled back into the kitchen and found him patting the chair beside him at the table. A stack of freshly laundered lab coats lay folded there.

"Oops. Forgot. Thanks, hon!" She grabbed the top one before finally focusing on Simon. He had laid out an elaborate map of what looked like the neighborhood and was making marks all over it.

She hesitated. "What is that?"

Simon studied her carefully. "A project. For school."

"You sure it's not a concilliabule?"

When he glanced up in surprise, Diane smiled. "Your word, hon. Secret meeting. Hatching plots?"

"Oh, yeah. I mean, this *is* for school."

Diane knew he wasn't lying. But she suspected he wasn't laying out the full truth either. Instead of flying out the door, she dropped into the chair beside him and brushed bits of cracked pepper off the tabletop.

"Looks cool. What class?" she asked.

Simon considered. "Life skills," he said at last.

"Okay." Diane leaned in closer. "I trust you. And you'll tell me if there's something I need to know. Right?"

Simon sighed. His mom had always protected him. But he didn't know how to go about protecting her. "You can trust me," he said.

"Want me to call Aunt Cathy? She can come over for the evening."

"Nah, I'm hanging out with Eric," Simon explained.

"Eric? Oh . . . I see." Now that she thought about it, Diane realized Simon had been spending quite a bit of time with Eric. His parents were good people. And Eric was always polite to her. "That's fine, sweetie," she added, scooting back from the table. "And I'm off all day Saturday, so we can hang out if you'd like. We'll make it fun."

Simon hoped he'd be ready for a victory celebration on Saturday and decided to go epic. "*Lord of the Rings RISK*, winner gets a whole bag of Pixie Sticks," he voted.

Diane kissed him on the top of his sandy curls. "I'm in." As she left, Simon called out, "Got a word?"

She paused in the doorway. "Yeah. I love you."

"I love you, too, Mom."

Diane smiled as she walked out the door.

* * *

Eric couldn't find his car keys. And that always made him feel claustrophobic. Cooped up. He rummaged through the mail on the kitchen counter as Lisa stacked plates in the dishwasher.

"You were really good last night," she said.

Eric froze in surprise. "You were there? At the concert?" His parents never came to his gigs. They liked his music fine, they said. But they heard enough of it pounding from the back shed.

Lisa rinsed crusted spaghetti sauce out of a saucepan. "Your dad was hoping to come too, but he got held up at work meeting a deadline."

Eric wasn't sure he believed her. He suspected Marcus just didn't like reminders of the music scene he'd once tried to break into.

"Why didn't I see you after—?" Eric began.

"There were so many people around you." Lisa's face was hidden as she bent over the dishwasher. "I didn't know . . . if you'd want me there."

"Oh." Eric had always assumed his parents stayed away as a silent protest against his drumming. But perhaps they really did feel out of place now. Unwanted. He wasn't quite sure what to do with that thought, so he shelved it. "Well, um . . . you should let me know next time. I could save you a seat. Seats."

She smiled. "If you don't mind; that would be nice."

"I gotta go. Snowglobe's playing at the riverfront."

It was true; he was late. Hurrying through the hall, he plunged out the front door—and nearly collided with Simon.

"Some people knock!" he said sharply.

"I was going to," Simon pointed out. "Until you came barging through."

Simon began unfolding a finely detailed map of the neighborhood. "We need to be really ready for tomorrow. I think we might need a backup to the backup plan," he tapped the school and then ran his finger up a side street. "How was it you climbed Annesdale Mansion?"

"Whoa," Eric shook his head. "This is getting out of control." He started down the front steps.

Simon scrambled to fold the map and follow. "We should meet up with the others and do a walk through."

Eric walked to the car, Simon at his heels. But as he reached the El Camino, he realized he hadn't found his keys. And he didn't feel like going back inside again.

"You have to know there's a million things that could go wrong." Shoving his hands in his pockets, Eric headed for the street. He'd walk to the riverfront. It was a hike, but it would help to clear his head. Besides, parking would be nearly impossible.

Simon trotted alongside, "That's exactly why we have to work out all the details! I mean, with Nick threatening to plant stuff in my locker—"

Eric whirled around. "He what? You didn't say anything about that!"

"It doesn't matter. We have to go to—"

"No!" Eric turned, picking up the pace. "Where you have to go is straight to your principal guy. Forget about Max. This is crazy."

"I can't!" It was the first time Eric had heard panic in Simon's voice.

"Why not?"

"Because." Simon's shorter legs struggled to keep up as his face flushed. "For starters, the principal is Mr. Matthews. And he has curly sandy hair. And he collects marbles. Especially the Swirls."

Eric slowed down, frowning. "So?"

"He grew up in Memphis. But moved away—twelve years ago."

"People do that," Eric commented.

"I'm twelve." Simon found himself pleading for Eric to understand everything he couldn't say. Everything he'd never said. Was he even right to trust Eric? But he couldn't stop the words from tumbling out. "I've always done this thing when I get nervous," he explained, rubbing his hand across his head front to back to demonstrate. "Mr. Matthews does it too."

Eric halted in the middle of the sidewalk and stared at him. "You can't possibly be saying what I think you're saying."

Simon waited.

"You really think . . ." Eric trailed off.

"Yeah," Simon's hands were shaking. Eric had never seen him like this.

"You think Mr. Matthews is your . . . ?"

Simon nodded.

"And Max . . . you think he's your . . ."

Simon nodded again, and Eric could see the relief in his face. But Eric couldn't help feeling like it was a long shot. Simon could easily be mistaken. It seemed more likely this guy with curly hair showed up and Simon invented a nice little story to make up for not having a dad around. Eric had never really considered what it might mean to Simon—not having a dad in the house. Eric so bitterly resented his own father, it didn't seem like much of a loss.

"Did you tell your mom this story?"

Simon's eyes widened in shock, and he shook his head. "I don't think she ever told him. Mr. Matthews, I mean."

Eric began walking again, as if motion could help sort this out.

"Hey!" Simon fell into step beside him as they turned up Bellevue. "I know where babies come from. And I'm pretty good at math."

Eric's head hurt. "So, you think your mom and Mr. Matthews . . ."

"They went to the same high school. They dated. I saw in her yearbook," Simon said in a rush. "I think they both started college at U of M. So it could have happened before he went up north to finish up at some fancy university. And she probably wanted to tell him in person, but then he shows up at Christmas with a fiancée—"

"And a kid on the way," Eric finished. "That's a nice story and all . . ."

"We look alike!" Simon pressed his case. "Our hair and how we move and everything."

"That's not exactly a DNA test."

"There's the marbles, too. I found a stash in Mom's drawer when I was four—all Swirls like this one." Simon held out the Joseph's Coat. "Mr. Matthews has a special jar in his office filled with antique Swirls. They're really rare!"

They'd reached the Lamar Avenue underpass. Someone had brought the dim space to life with portraits of Memphis music legends. Isaac Hayes, Otis Redding, Johnny Taylor, all the greats who'd played on Stax Records. Eric stared at the faces, wishing he was down at the riverfront, lost in the beat. Instead of lost in this tangled drama with Simon.

"Okay, the marble thing is weird. For both of you," Eric added, finally cracking a smile. "Let's say it's true. Let's say that Mr. Matthews is your dad. Why don't you just tell him everything?"

"Just tell him I think I'm the son he never knew he had?" Simon asked in disbelief. Maybe telling Eric was a mistake after all.

"No," Eric corrected. "Just about Nick and Max and the Reaper and all this business with the database scam."

Simon nodded, more confident now they had returned to the point. "I can't prove anything. I mean, nothing big. The teachers think Nick is perfect. He'll pin the whole thing on Max. And Max will hate me forever. Besides, it puts Mr. Matthews in a bad spot. What's he supposed to do with a cheating scandal right when the auditor is on campus—"

"Maybe telling Eric was a mistake after all."

Simon's a weird kid, Eric couldn't help thinking. But it was a good kind of weird, like looking at someone who'd grown up faster inside than out. Eric took a deep breath and turned away from a portrait of Al Green. If Simon wouldn't go to his mom or Mr. Matthews, well . . . he needed someone. "Yeah, okay."

"Max already hates it here," Simon pressed on. "And if Nick—"

"Okay!" Eric shouted. His voiced echoed, hollowed out by the underpass. "I said I'll do it! I'll help with your crazy plan."

"Oh. Thanks."

Eric was surprised to see Simon go limp with relief. The kid was actually counting on him. "So you'd better clue me in on the rest of it," he added.

Simon snapped back into business mode. "Right. Well, to start with, you should have these in case you need them." He handed over a small bag of marbles as they began the walk home. "Now, I'm supposed to meet Nick at Mr. Matthews' office, right at 6:45 sharp."

Rocking out to Snowglobe would have to wait.

FRIDAY

As Eric crossed over the railroad tracks with Marcus and Lisa, he spotted the crowd ahead on the Annesdale Middle campus. If you'd told him a week ago he'd be saving a bunch of middle school kids from a cheating scandal, he wouldn't have believed you. But it felt kind of good to think about someone else's future for a change.

"Everything okay?" Marcus asked. He'd actually ditched an editorial workshop today. And for once, his words didn't sound like an accusation.

"I'm good," Eric assured him. "I said I'd hang out with Simon some. You know, since his mom couldn't come and all."

Eric waited for their objection, but it didn't come. They continued in silence as they crossed the campus; the old warehouse didn't really look like a school. Food stalls and a student art fair crowded around three sides of the building, and canned music pumped through the air.

Return to sender, address unknown
No such number, no such zone . . .

—crooned The King. Eric wondered if his role in this makeshift operation would really help Simon. *What if he was just making things worse?* But then he spotted Michael waving from across the lawn. There was no backing out now.

"Weren't those kids at your concert?" Lisa asked. "Who's that?"

"Elvis," Eric responded. "Long story. Look, I'll see you later." He began weaving through the crowd, leaving his parents to puzzle it out. As he neared the stage, a tall man with tight sandy curls climbed up and took the microphone. Eric stopped in his tracks; that had to be the principal. And he *did* look *a lot* like Simon.

Mr. Matthews signaled to a sound tech, and the music faded out as he addressed the crowd. "Welcome to Annesdale Middle!" he greeted them. "As always, we are grateful for the support of neighbors like you. It's been a fantastic two years, and we're already seeing extraordinary results. Today, I'm pleased to introduce you to Mr. Gerlich." He waved toward a small man who looked out of place in a starchy suit. "He's been evaluating our progress and will be renewing the school's charter as we prepare for the years ahead. So be extra friendly if you meet him," Mr. Matthews joked.

Eric tuned out as Mr. Matthews continued with something about educational reform. Where was Simon? Eric squeezed past a stall that showcased an entire hog, meat literally falling off the bone. He resisted temptation and pressed around the edge of the crowd.

There, ahead, he spotted Simon tailing a tall, blonde kid with a messenger bag and cap who could only be Nick. The boy to his right, a head shorter but muscular, must be Brody. And the dark-haired kid between them had to be Max.

Mr. Matthews was finishing up onstage. "I'll be back in half an hour to give an update on our fundraising efforts. Until then, enjoy the day and don't forget to stop by the art fair," he added.

"Some of our very talented students have created original pieces for this occasion. You never know what they will be worth one day; we may have the next Carroll Cloar in our midst! So if you believe in Annesdale, now's your time to prove it and place a bid."

Did Mr. Matthews know what some of his very talented students were pulling off right now? Eric wondered as he took up position between the barbecue stall and a face-painting tent to await his signal.

★ ★ ★

Simon checked his phone as Mr. Matthews started down from the stage: 6:38. Seven minutes to go. He patted his pocket once more to make sure the all-important piece of paper was still there. Nearby, Dwayne and Michael shifted to keep a clear view of Nick, while Anna moved into place near the stage steps. Quickly, Simon circled around the crowd and slipped up behind Mr. Matthews, just as Anna popped into the principal's path.

"Mr. Matthews?" She beamed, tossing her long hair and holding out a hand.

"That's me—" he shook her hand, but Anna was already chattering a mile a minute.

"I go to Bellevue Middle, but I have friends here and the way you do classes is *so* cool! I mean, it's not like every kid learns exactly the same way so it only makes sense to switch it up. . . ."

Simon could see from the tilt of Mr. Matthews' head that he was listening, bemused and a little distracted. It was just the moment Simon needed to slip two fingers into Mr. Matthews' back pocket and nab his phone. He'd practiced so many times last night on Eric that he was pretty sure Mr. Matthews' didn't notice a thing.

The second he had the phone free and clear, he left Anna to

work herself out of the conversation and slid through the crowd to the side of the face-painting tent. Here, in the bushes, he was completely hidden as he set to work on Mr. Matthews' phone and the app he needed to download.

Simon had left the other kids to be his eyes and ears on Nick and Brody, but he was in luck. They were outside the tent, and if he tried, he could just make out their conversation through the scrubby leaves.

Nick, as usual, had gathered a crowd of half-admiring, half-fearful underclassmen. "Finals," he taunted, "aren't like your average test. They can ruin you. When you're not endowed with my kind of cerebral capabilities, that is." Turning to Brody, he laughed. "They don't even know what I just said."

One red-headed sixth grader dared to speak up. "What *does* that mean?"

"It means," Nick taunted, "when you're about to pee yourself because you screwed up your finals—come to me. For a little investment on your part, I'll be able to do something about it." As the kids gaped at him, Nick nudged Brody and thwacked Max on the shoulder. "C'mon, Mama. We got work to do."

As they turned to go, Simon saw Nick reach up to touch his cap—but it wasn't on his head. Frowning, Nick checked his bag; the hat was there. He shrugged and pulled it out. But as Nick slid it onto his head, Simon saw something extraordinary happen. Out of the cap rained a storm of green powder. It covered Nick's hair and poured across his face. It coated his white shirt.

"How the—" Nick spluttered, dabbing frantically at the powder. Rubbing made it worse. Green streaks highlighted his cheeks and dyed his shirt, his hands.

Simon craned his neck for a better view, then checked Mr.

Matthews' phone. Still downloading. Mr. Matthews needed to switch cell phone carriers.

A few suppressed giggles rose from the crowd around Nick as he scrubbed at the green mess. He glared at them. "All right, who did it?!"

A voice piped up from the back of the group. Simon saw it was Dwayne. "Dude. *You* just pulled it out of your bag."

Seething, Nick yanked that cap low over his face. He turned his back to the kids and hauled Brody several steps away from Max, talking in a low voice. Simon could no longer hear their conversation, but Nick was near Eric—so Simon would have to trust in Eric for now.

Simon checked the phone again. In movies, the hero could download important files in seconds. But the status bar told him this would take another *eighteen* minutes. And his watch told him it was 6:43. He would just have to pray the app kept loading—and that Mr. Matthews had no reason to check his phone.

When he glanced up again, Nick was heading for the school's side entrance—but Brody and Max had taken off in the opposite direction. Simon's mind raced. He needed Max to stay with Nick. He needed to get this phone back to Mr. Matthews. He needed—

A hand locked onto his arm, and Simon jumped. It was Eric.

"Change of plans," Eric told him brusquely before Simon could ask. "They're holding Max hostage to make sure you follow through. Somehow, Nick got the impression you care what happens to Max."

"We have to get Max—" Simon darted forward, but Eric tugged him back.

"Brody's taking him to Elmwood."

"What?"

"Brody wanted to stash him in the school, but Nick thought he'd scream or something. They're using one of the crypts."

Frantic, Simon checked the phone. Seventeen minutes. "I have to get to Max!"

"No, you have to get to Nick. We've got Max covered." Simon glanced around and caught a glimpse of Michael, Dwayne, and Anna unearthing their stashed backpacks. He started to protest again, but Eric shook his head. "Don't worry. We'll make it back in time for our gig."

Simon had made a choice three days ago to trust Eric. Now wasn't the time to stop. "All right," he said. "And I need something else, too." He flashed Mr. Matthews' phone. "Someone's got to get this back in Mr. Matthews' pocket—but only *after* the app finishes downloading."

"Dude. Got it!" Dwayne snaked out his hand for the phone, but Simon held it back. "I need to know how long I have to stall." Quickly, he synched a timer on his own phone. Then he handed Mr. Matthews' phone to Eric.

What was happening to Max? Eric must have sensed Simon's fear, because he placed a hand on Simon's shoulder. "It'll be okay. I'll text you updates. Let me know if you run into trouble, okay?"

Nodding, Simon brushed debris from the bushes off his jeans and took off for the side entrance as Eric and the kids headed toward the railroad tracks.

Sixteen minutes to go.

Simon knew that Nick's vanity would call for a trip to the

bathroom first, despite their appointed meeting time at Mr. Matthews' office. So Simon had already taken up a position in the empty hallway behind a stand banner when Nick emerged from the bathroom—still green, and now soaking wet.

The older boy stormed directly to his locker. Another telltale photograph taped to the front spelled out the full story: a close up of Nick, smartphone in hand, posting on Facebook under the malevolent red eyes of AMS Reaper.

Nick the Reaper.

Nick ripped the image in two and yanked open his locker door, looking for something.

Whatever it was, he didn't find it.

Cursing under his breath, he slammed his locker door and hurried off down the hall and around the corner.

Simon forced himself to count to thirty before checking the timer on his phone again. *Twelve minutes to go.* He would have to buy some extra time.

Slipping out from behind the banner, Simon sauntered down the hall. When he turned the corner, he spied Nick, pacing impatiently in front of Mr. Matthews' office.

"You're late!" Nick barked.

"And you're a little green," Simon commented.

"Shut up." Nick stalked closer. "Where's the code?"

Simon stood his ground and reached into his pocket. He wanted to check the time on his phone, but he couldn't do that now. Not with Nick watching. Instead, his fingers snagged the folded

paper with the code—at the same time rolling his Swirl into his palm like a security blanket.

Simon pulled out the page, clasped between his thumb and forefinger, the marble secure in his palm.

He had made sure to print the code rather than simply handing over a text file on a thumb drive. If Nick wasn't smart enough to code it himself, Simon wanted to watch Nick painstakingly type each character.

"It's . . . right here."

Nick pounced, swiping for the paper. Simon stepped back just in time. "I just . . . I don't know . . . I don't think I can go through with this." He left the paper dangling there, inches from Nick's hand.

"You should have thought of that sooner." Nick smirked and dove for the paper once more. Simon snapped it out of his reach again, but as he did so, lost his grip on the marble. It thudded against the floor and rolled down the hall, the colors swirling wildly—

Simon froze. He couldn't leave it. But Nick was already lunging after him.

Simon ran.

He skidded around one corner after another, Nick's feet pounding after him. He knew he couldn't outrun Nick for long and was thankful for the crash bar just ahead. Slamming through the back door, he cut across the lot north of the cemetery, Nick still in hot pursuit. The paper with the code seemed to burn, balled up in his right palm.

Simon hoped that Eric and his friends had made it into the cemetery all right, but he couldn't spare them more than a second's thought as he bee-lined under the highway and over the railroad

tracks. Turning up Bellevue, he cast a quick glance behind him. Nick was closing in with silent, steely determination.

Had they found Max? Or was Max locked up right now in one of the cold stone vaults with the sun sinking low? Heart thudding, Simon tugged out his phone with his left hand and stole a glance down at the screen. Time was betraying him: slowing down, holding him hostage to *nine more long minutes.*

Simon's toe caught on a crack in the sidewalk. For one frantic moment, he saw the pavement rising to meet him, ready to smack him in the face.

He couldn't lose the code! Instead, he shot out his left arm to break the fall—

And landed hard on the rough cement. Something shattered. Simon rolled to his side and dared to look: his arm was only scraped up. But his phone was smashed beyond repair. A blank screen told him the timer was gone. His connection to Eric and Max was slashed. And Nick was just yards away, bearing down fast.

Staggering to his feet, Simon forced himself to run again. He tilted right onto Agnes, making a dash for the grounds of Annesdale Mansion; he wanted no witnesses to what he must do next. But as he plunged into the azalea thicket on the south side, a hand gripped his arm like a vice. Nick.

Simon wasn't ready to give in yet. Holding up the crumpled paper, he glared at Nick. "Try to touch this, and I'll tear it up!"

Now that he had the upper hand, Nick had regained his cool. "You think I can't make you give that to me?" he smirked, releasing Simon's arm.

Simon faced Nick as an equal. "You don't have to do this."

Nick smirked. "Oh, I get it. Now that you're down, you've got a special moral code."

Simon didn't flinch. "It's not just grades. You're compromising Social Security numbers and stuff like that. You should get out now."

"So Simon says," Nick drawled. "But *you're* the one who wrote this code. I may ace everything else, but I'm only average in Computer Applications. Everyone knows that."

Simon gripped the paper in both hands. "I won't do it!"

"Really?" Casually, Nick leaned over so he was on Simon's level. "See, I know you've got this little thing for Mama . . . Max, you know. I can't imagine why. But, well, Brody's got him right now. And if you don't hand me that paper in the next fifteen seconds . . ." Nick savored the moment. "Max gets a beat down, and both of you get busted for hacking in."

Simon didn't have to manufacture the fear in his eyes. If Eric hadn't come through, Max was in big trouble. They all were. He gave himself a full fifteen seconds. Then slowly, he handed over the paper.

Triumphant, Nick unfolded it and checked the page of closely typed commands. "You're not off the hook until it works, Smith. Got that?"

Simon nodded and closed his eyes. When he opened them moments later, Nick was gone. He had no way of knowing if Max was safe. If Mr. Matthews had his phone back.

Simon wracked his brain trying to remember what the countdown clock had shown just before it smashed. He tried to visualize the time. How many minutes? As he hightailed it back to school along Sledge Avenue, he hoped there were enough.

* * *

The sun hung low in the western sky, while in the east, a pale moon was already visible. Every statue in the cemetery pushed a long, spidery shadow across the grass. Max was sure he saw them moving. Whispering. His only comfort was that Brody seemed to hate the place as much as he did.

"Move it!" Brody hissed, shoving Max ahead of him.

Max saw it in a flash of comprehension: there had never been a chance of being part of Nick's inner circle. Even Brody wasn't in. The only one who would ever benefit from association with Nick . . . was Nick.

"You're kidnapping me, right?" he flustered.

"You don't know anything," Brody snarled.

Max tried to twist away, but Brody's grip was like iron, steering him past Celtic crosses and weeping angels and tiny oval graves that Max was certain must belong to children. Brody seemed rattled, and Max was pretty sure they had wandered in circles for at least ten minutes before Brody finally slowed the pace, peering at a street sign in the fading light. Where were they, Max wondered: the corner of Fear and Loathing?

Then he turned, and saw it: a mausoleum. Its swooping peaked roof and carved cornerstones were straight from a horror film

"C'mon," Brody grunted, towing him toward the entrance.

Max felt a sudden rush of panic, like ice moving through his veins, freezing his arms and legs. He hadn't really believed Brody would leave him here. Alone. "You're putting me in *there*?" he whispered.

"Max felt a
sudden rush
of panic."

"If I leave you out here, you'll scream, right?" Still gripping Max's shirt with one hand, Brody yanked a small crowbar from his pocket and began prying open the door of the crypt. Max made another desperate attempt to twist free. It was fruitless, but he did discover one thing; Brody's hands were shaking.

"You're scared, too!" Max accused, desperate.

Brody tried to laugh. "Scared of what? Stupid dead people?"

That's when Max saw the zombie. It was perched at the peak of the roof, just over Brody's head.

"Z . . . z . . . zom . . ." Max didn't have enough air to get any further, but the terror in his face was clear. Brody swung around. The zombie flung itself off the roof, knocking Brody to the ground, breaking his grip on Max's shirt.

Brody shrieked, just as two more walking dead swarmed around the sides of the vault. Max fled. He made it only a short way down the lane before a tall, dark figure loomed up before him. Max started to scream, but the figure placed a hand over his mouth.

"Hey, it's okay! Simon sent us."

"He sent *zombies*?" Max croaked, muffled.

"I'm Eric, they're . . . never mind. Here. You can help." Eric released Max and pressed a dozen marbles into Max's palm. Automatically, Max locked his fingers around them, and they both turned back to the fray. The zombies had begun with the advantage of surprise, but Brody outweighed them all. Driven by panic, he shook the trio off and sprinted straight toward Max and Eric.

"Go!" shouted Eric, releasing a battery of marbles. Max stood frozen as Brody dodged the marbles, clearing the minefield and sprinting for freedom.

"Max!" Eric called. Snapping to attention, Max hurled his marbles ahead. They sprayed around Brody's feet. The bully sidestepped, tripped, and went down once more in the grass. Max heard a smattering of applause behind him. Someone shouted, "Well done!" and for a moment, Max basked in the glow of their approval.

Brody recovered quickly, and the band of zombies chased after him, moaning and shrieking in their best impersonations of the undead. Driven by sheer terror, Brody soon outpaced them and disappeared into the gathering darkness just as Eric caught up.

"I wanted to put him in the river!" bemoaned a dark-haired zombie.

"Nah." Eric grinned. "We got Max. And Brody's heading the wrong direction anyway."

"He got lost bringing me in here," Max added, pleased that his voice didn't squeak. "This place is like a maze!"

"Wicked." Dwayne punched Max on the shoulder. "We'll leave that fool to the ghouls."

★ ★ ★

As Eric shepherded his ragtag crew through the fence on the north side of the cemetery, he wondered how long it would take Brody to find his way back. He hoped it wouldn't interfere with Simon's plan—but then, their original strategy had been shot to pieces, anyway.

Eric glanced over at Max; his face was pink with pleased embarrassment as Anna pointed out how she'd done her zombie makeup.

"C'mon!" Eric prodded them along. "It's not over yet!" He'd texted Simon about Max, but there was no response. He hoped the kid was okay.

"How much time we got left?" Dwayne demanded, and Eric did another check of Mr. Matthews' phone. "Two minutes," he announced. "Let's move it!"

The zombies drew some curious eyes as they plunged back into the crowd at the festival and worked their way toward the stage. "The face painting this year is really quite extraordinary!" he overheard one lavender-haired old lady exclaim. Eric spied his parents chatting with Mr. Matthews and the school auditor as they checked out the student art fair. They stared, open-mouthed, at his entourage, but Eric only waved. Mr. Matthews' phone was burning a hole in his pocket.

"Dude, is it done already?" Dwayne was nearly exploding with energy. The zombie trio and Max gathered around as Eric pulled out the phone again. The status bar zinged the final fraction and the phone *dinged* loudly. Download complete.

"Hey!" Max frowned. "Is that my dad's phone?"

Eric's brain sizzled as he tried to sort out what Max needed to know. "Look, Simon's got it under control," he began, hoping it was true. "He can put a stop to Nick and Brody, and make sure you come out of this with a clean record. But the whole thing is going to be a lot easier if you can be straight with your dad and just tell him what's going on."

Max's eyes widened. "I . . . I can't do that!"

Eric took a deep breath and forced himself to slow down. "You'll be helping yourself. And Simon." The zombies were closing ranks around Max, supportive. "All of us."

"But . . ." Max's eyes scanned the crowd. Mr. Matthews was working his way toward the stage.

"We've gotta move. Your dad is going to head for his office very soon. Just wait inside the school, and then follow him into his office."

"I . . . okay," Max's voice wavered. He slowly turned and headed toward the school, twisting to look over his shoulder every few moments—as if Brody might be waiting to snatch him again.

Eric hoped the kid would follow through, but he had no time to think about it.

Anna stood on her tiptoes, peering through the mass of bodies. "He's coming this way. Give me the phone!"

"No." Dwayne surveyed the layout of the stage area. "Check out that big magnolia tree. I'll climb up and then slide way out onto that branch. Michael, you get him right under it by singing *You Ain't Nothin' But a Hound Dog*. And while he's standing there trying to figure out The King's return, I'll hang upside down off the branch and drop it in his back pocket." Dwayne popped the phone out of Eric's hand to demonstrate.

"Not *Hound Dog*," Michael argued. "*Blue Suede Shoes* is better."

"Actually," Anna jumped in, "since I've already done this once, I think I should get him to explain his philosophy of education and—"

"Gimme that." Eric nabbed the phone back from Dwayne and sauntered directly toward the principal. He could feel the tension from the zombies at his back.

"Mr. Matthews?" he called and held up the device. "Is this your phone?"

Mr. Matthews blinked and took the phone. "Yes, it is. I didn't think . . . I must have set it down. Thank you, Mr.—"

Eric demonstrated his firm handshake. "Eric Rogers. Friend of Simon Smith. I think you were just talking with Lisa . . . with my mom and dad."

"Oh, yes. It's great to have the support of our neighbors! Now, if you'll excuse me, I need to give another update." Mr. Matthews hurried up to the stage.

Eric turned back to the zombies, who were staring at him open mouthed. He shrugged. "I like to keep it simple." When they didn't move, he beckoned them closer. "Get ready. Our real gig could start any second."

Nerves strung tight with expectation, they all turned to the stage. Once again, Mr. Matthews silenced the crowd. "I have to say again what a pleasure it is to have such an incredible turnout today. Y'all are going above and beyond. I just heard that our student art fair has already reached their fundraising goal, and—"

A loud beeping interrupted him. He twisted, looking for the source until he realized it was coming from his own pocket. Red-faced, he pulled out his phone. "I'm sorry about that. If you'll just—"

But instead of silencing his phone, Mr. Matthews gaped at the tiny screen. The moment stretched out, awkward. Eric could sense the crowd shifting uncomfortably. Mr. Gerlich, the auditor, frowned and edged up toward the stage.

With a quick nod to the zombies, Eric zipped smoothly to the stage, cutting off the auditor. Skipping the steps, he hoisted himself up and stood beside Mr. Matthews. He cleared his throat.

"Uh, Mr. Matthews just wanted to let you know he'll have the

rest of those numbers soon. . . ." Eric smiled at the principal and nodded knowingly toward the building.

Mr. Matthews jerked back to attention. "Yes!" he sputtered. "I'll just be right back." Eyes still glued to his phone, Mr. Matthews stumbled off the stage and headed for the school.

It appeared Mr. Gerlich might follow, but Eric waved for attention again. "And in the meantime, we have a special surprise for you." Michael and Dwayne hauled a metal trashcan up on stage, and Anna stepped boldly up to a second mic as Eric continued, "A little live entertainment from a new local group I like to call . . . *The Zombies!*"

Pulling out his drumsticks, he laid down an opening beat on the trashcan lid. Mr. Gerlich stopped in his tracks and watched, bemused, as the zombies launched into song.

★ ★ ★

Simon needed to sneeze. Maybe he was allergic to azaleas. Whatever the case, he couldn't possibly sneeze right now because he was wedged tightly behind the armchair in Mr. Matthews' office.

The dim room was entirely silent, except for the excited tapping of Nick's fingers on Mr. Matthews' computer keyboard.

It had been surprisingly easy to sneak into the room. Nick was so intent on deciphering Simon's code that he had left the door unlocked. Simon had simply crawled in, slithering into position as Nick exalted over the page of neat programming commands.

Should he have waited for Max? But he didn't even know if Eric and the zombies had managed to free Max. Simon shook his head and squeezed the tip of his nose to contain the threatening sneeze. He clutched an envelope from his locker in the other hand.

Pounding footsteps sounded in the hallway, and the door flung open. For one moment, Simon thought it was Max. But his sneak peek revealed that it was Brody, wide-eyed and wild-haired. "Nick! They got him," Brody croaked. Instantly, Nick sprang for the door. He shut and locked it before swinging back to face Brody.

"Keep a lid on it! We're in, okay?"

"They took Max. These crazy zombies attacked me and I got lost—"

Behind the chair, Simon grinned. Max was free! But he needed Max here, right now—

"Zombies in the graveyard." Nick smirked. "Right. So you freaked out and let him go. Well, it doesn't matter. We've got the code—and we've got enough on Mama and the Smith kid that they're screwed if they ever talk."

Nick dropped back down in front of the computer again. "Just look at this! A shadow login. We're almost in . . . this should do it." Checking Simon's coded page, he clicked a few more keys and hit "Enter." "There!" he exalted. "Look at that!"

"What am I looking at?" Brody frowned.

Nick laughed. "Seriously? You're looking at the foundation of an empire here. Grades. Home addresses. Emails. Everything we need for a middle-school black market. We can run this thing for years."

"But . . ." Brody pondered, "We won't be here next year."

"Well, *you'll* be here unless we tweak your grades," Nick pointed out, "but I'm getting out for sure. That's the beauty of the whole thing. We work remotely, in the dark, no one suspects us!"

The overhead light flared on as the door flew open, banging against the wall.

"Mr. Darby!" Mr. Matthews stormed into his office. "Care to tell me what's going on here?"

He held up his phone. The screen showed live, real-time video of Nick and Brody—streaming directly from the camera on Mr. Matthews' computer to the app Simon had installed.

Brody froze, but Nick quickly smoothed over his panic with a look of deep concern. "Mr. Matthews, I realize how this looks—"

"Yes, like you poured green dye all over yourself—"

Nick winced.

"And then broke into my office and accessed my computer!"

"It's just . . . well, it's about Max."

Simon saw Mr. Matthews stiffen. *Where was Max? What if he'd chickened out? Surely Eric had made it clear how important this was.*

"Max." Mr. Matthews crossed his arm, wary.

"He came to me last week and told me he'd stolen a key to your office so he could make a profit charging kids to change their exam grades. He wanted my help. I tried so hard to talk him out of it." Nick paused, dramatically.

"Go on." Mr. Matthews' voice was even. It gave nothing away.

"I couldn't do it. Max broke in, but I knew he made a mess of it. I didn't want him getting in trouble, so I begged him to let me have the key so I could come in and cover his tracks. Wipe the slate

clean, so to speak. Let him start over."

Mr. Matthews stared Nick down, hard. "Is this true?"

"It is, sir."

"Mr. Darby, we have to face that however good your motives, you have just hacked into the school's database."

Simon couldn't fight the sneeze any longer. It exploded from his body, rocking the chair. Everyone gaped as he shot up from behind the chair.

"Actually," Simon said. "He hasn't."

Mr. Matthews was at a loss. "Simon! What on earth?"

Simon stepped out from behind the chair with a sharp glance at the door. This was all happening too fast. "Nick hasn't hacked into the school database. He's only accessed a dummy database."

Nick's façade broke. "Why you little—" He fought to recover his polish. "It doesn't matter. My only misdemeanor, if you can call it that, is helping out Max."

"No."

The soft voice jerked every eye in the room toward the door. Max stood there, pale but determined. Simon nearly wilted with relief. "Max!" Mr. Matthews exclaimed. "Now is not—"

Max kept his eyes fixed on Nick. "No. I was the one who helped *you*. But you don't even care. I never should have done it."

Nick's lip curled. "See, Mr. Matthews? He still can't tell you the truth, even now. All he can do is blame me." Nick was playing it up now. "It really hurts. I mean, the poor kid has no friends, and I've

tried over and over to help him feel at home here! I've—"

It was too much. "Really, Nick?" Simon tossed his envelope onto the desk and waited until he caught Nick's eye. Then he dropped a used green dye packet on top of the envelope. "Helping kids like Max. Is that what you've been doing? *Really?*"

Nick's face paled under its green streaks. He didn't need to open the envelope to know what was inside: undeniable photographic evidence of Nick, the AMS Reaper. For once, he was wordless.

"Would *someone* please—" breaking off, Mr. Matthews took Max by the shoulders and pulled him forward. "Simon, explain what's going on. Or all four of you are suspended, pending administrative review!"

Simon took a deep breath. He knew he held all the cards. But he still had to play them in the right order. "Let's suppose," he began, "that a couple guys want to bust into the school database and start a black market in grades . . . just when the school's charter is on the line." His eyes nailed Nick and Brody.

Mr. Matthews' eyes narrowed. "I want facts, Mr. Smith. Not hypotheticals."

"Please!" Simon could feel his fingernails digging into his palms. "Just hear me out! This story is going somewhere. I promise."

After a brief moment, Mr. Matthews nodded. "It better get there fast."

"Okay." Simon tried to recover his thoughts. "Suppose you've got these guys trying to hack in. And then suppose one of those guys has a stellar reputation, because he's managed to hide what he's up to and always recruits someone else to do his dirty work— someone like the principal's son, who's new in town."

Mr. Matthews glanced down at Max, comprehension dawning.

Simon's hand slid into his pocket, searching for his Joseph's Coat marble. He remembered, with a stab of loss, that it was missing. But he had to keep going. "And let's pretend this guy with the awesome reputation needs someone to crack the computer code for him. He blackmails someone to help him. But that someone wants to put a stop to the whole thing once and for all—"

Mr. Matthews cleared his throat. "Pronouns aside—why didn't this 'someone' come directly to me?"

Simon held his gaze. "Well, the guy who's running it all needs to know he can never pull anything like this again. Ever. So, the guy who got blackmailed . . . well, he needs evidence. *Needed* evidence." He allowed his eyes to drift toward the envelope on the desk. Mr. Matthews' eyes followed, too.

Simon could feel Nick's burning rage. He knew the older boy was desperate to snatch away the envelope. But even to touch it would be to acknowledge it was important.

Slowly, Mr. Matthews stepped toward his desk. Ignoring Nick's glare, he picked up the envelope and took his time to cinch open the flap without tearing it. Simon was pretty sure no one else in the room was breathing as the principal studied the photos inside, one at a time. Finally, he glanced up—face impassive. "Is this the whole story?"

"Simon knows Photoshop!" blurted Nick. "So what?"

"I was speaking to Mr. Smith," Mr. Matthews told him coolly and turned back to Simon.

"Well, there's the principal's son," Simon added. "I mean, in this story. He has to find out first that he *wants* to get out of the whole thing." Simon dared a quick glance at Max who, for once,

didn't flinch.

"And what about this hypothetical school charter on the line?" Mr. Matthews sounded grim. But Simon thought he could detect the faintest trace of a smile.

"Supposing it all went down this way, there's been no cheating. There's been nothing illegal," Simon pointed out.

"Just a little case of breaking and entering . . . and some other matters I'll be researching," Mr. Matthews said, frowning at Nick and Brody.

"I'm sure the principal would have ways to deal with that," Simon suggested. "Hypothetically speaking." He stole a glance at Max and gave him a quick thumbs up, down low.

After a long moment, Mr. Matthews released Max and stepped over to his desk. "Well, Simon," he said. "I hope you're getting A's in English for your storytelling skills." He turned to Nick and Brody. "Mr. Darby, Mr. Jones, I expect to see you in here first thing on Monday morning to discuss the ending to this story." When Nick and Brody didn't move he commanded, "You're done for the day!"

Brody slouched for the door, but Nick fired one last dart. "Why would you ever trust Smith? He has no proof but some doctored photos—"

Simon plucked the dye packet from the desk and handed it to Nick. "You don't want to forget this," he reminded. "Green really does something for you."

Nick glared, but he knew he'd been beaten. He stalked out the door after Brody.

Mr. Matthews placed his hand briefly on Max's shoulder. "Go ahead, Max. We'll talk later." His voice was stern, but not unkind.

As Max left, he finally turned to Simon. "You've broken at least three school rules here. But that aside, I can't understand why you would go to all this trouble for Max. And, I think . . . for me."

Simon swallowed hard. "It's just . . . I was trying to figure out what would make the best story. Sir."

"I see," Mr. Matthews said. And Simon thought that, just maybe, he did. Simon turned for the door, but Mr. Matthews called after him.

"What's that at your feet?" he asked. Simon glanced down. There, resting against the door frame, was his Joseph's Coat marble. Relief flooded through Simon as he picked it up and placed it in his palm where the light caught the spinning colors.

"It's my shooter marble, sir. I lost it."

Mr. Matthews stared at the marble for a long moment. Then he glanced at his own jar of Swirls. At last he said, "I used to have a Swirl just like that one. Until I gave it away."

Simon smiled. "Yessir."

Then he pushed open the door and left the office.

★ ★ ★

Eric smiled as he watched the tribe of zombies surround Max. It looked like the kid would be wanting his own undead makeup soon.

Lisa handed her son a barbecue sandwich as Marcus thumped Eric on the back. "Glad I could finally see you perform," he commented. "You want me to write up a review?"
"In the real estate section?" Eric quipped through a mouthful

of sauce.

"I thought I'd see if the paper will let me get back to moonlighting a few music reviews here and there," Marcus noted, smiling. "Where'd you get the singing zombies?"

"Eric photographed their musical debut last weekend," a friendly voice answered. "Looks like he's really launched their careers." Eric turned to see Ken, camera around his neck, barbecue in hand.

Ken offered his free hand to Marcus, and Eric made quick introductions. "I might help Ken with his group this summer," he explained, before considering his words—and then hurried to course correct. "I mean, if I've got time after the Drum Shop. And maybe a class or two."

Eric could tell his parents were pleased, but they were smart enough not to push it. Instead, Lisa pointed toward the school. "I think Simon's looking for you." Eric spun around. Sure enough, Simon was zipping toward them, and his face read victory. Eric released a long breath he hadn't even realized he was holding.

"Everything okay with Simon?" Ken asked softly.

"Better be after all this—" Eric broke off; his parents were watching, curious.

"Of course Simon's fine. He's . . . he has . . ." Marcus' voice was a little gruff as he searched for the right words. "He's got Eric looking out for him."

Eric didn't dare look at his father, but he felt something unknot, deep inside. "Better go see what Simon wants." He turned to Ken and added, "Text me when you want me at Crump's studio to record, okay?"

"I used to
have a Swirl
just like that
one. Until
I gave it
away."

* * *

Later, as the festival wound down and faded into the humid evening, Simon and Max debriefed with the zombies under the magnolia tree. Eric hauled the trashcan he'd used for their performance back to its proper spot and clanged the lid into place. It had been a rush, but he was glad to put a cap on this evening. As he turned, he was surprised to find Mr. Matthews at his elbow.

"Eric, right?" the principal asked.

"That's me," Eric stole a glance at Simon and the kids. "Found your phone."

Mr. Matthews smiled, wry. "Something like that." His eyes followed Eric's gaze. "You know Simon pretty well?"

"Sure. He lives next door. I give him drumming lessons."

Mr. Matthews considered. "He's an interesting kid."

"Yeah. Interesting and complicated." Eric shifted uncomfortably. "But he's a good kid to know."

"Any suggestions for how I'd get to know him?" Mr. Matthews asked.

"Well," Eric paused for a moment and glanced across the lot at Simon—who grinned back. "He likes to play marbles."

A LOT CAN HAPPEN
IN A WEEK . . .

So—look around. Who are the Simons and Erics in your world? Maybe you can even spot a Max or two. Whether you know it or not, you have a role to play in their stories. But time is moving fast. Soon, your turn will be up. The week will end. So what are you doing to make this week count? Are you ready to start playing for keeps?

this side up

FLIP ME OVER
TO READ
**PLAYING FOR
KEEPS**

this side up

FLIP ME OVER
TO READ
**LOSING YOUR
MARBLES**

WORKS CITED

Tribes Over Time

[1] Amanda Enayati, "The Importance of Belonging," *CNNHealth*, online: http://www.cnn.com/2012/06/01/health/enayati-importance-of-belonging (Accessed April 4, 2013).

[2] Jane Howard, ThinkExist, http://thinkexist.com/quotation/call_it_a_clan-call_it_a_network-call_it_a_tribe/323634.html

[3] Seth Godin, "The Tribes We Lead." Filmed February 2009, TEDvideo 17:27. Posted May 2009. http://www.ted.com/talks/seth_godin_on_the_tribes_we_lead.html.

[4] Geoffrey Canada, *Reaching Up for Manhood: Transforming the Lives of Boys in America* (Boston: Beacon Press, 1998).

[5] Luc Reid, *Talk the Talk* (New York: Fall River Press, 2006), 1.

[6] Nancy Gibbs, "The Magic of the Family Meal," *Time Magazine.* Online: June 4, 2006, http://www.time.com/time/magazine/article/0,9171,1200760,00.html#ixzz2PMryiQNP (accessed April 2013).

[7] Ibid.

Fun Over Time

[1] Ps. 68:3, Phil. 4:4, Eccl. 3:4, Ex 10:9, Prov. 17:22, Ps. 100:2, Gal. 5:22, Acts 2:46, Eccl. 11:8.

[2] Stuart Brown, "Play is More Fun." Filmed May 2008, TEDvideo. Posted March 2009. http://www.ted.com/talks/stuart_brown_says_play_is_more_than_fun_it_s_vital.html

[3] Lawrence J. Cohen, Ph.D, *Playful Parenting* (New York: Ballantine Books, 2002), 17.

[4] ibid.

[5] Rom 12:8

[6] Harriet Lerner PhD, *The Dance of Connection,* (New York Harper Collins, 2001), xiii

[7] *Hook,* dir. by Steven Spielburg (1991; Sony Pictures, 2000 DVD).

[8] Regina Berreca, "The Secret Behind Women's Laughter," *Psychology Today*, January 9, 2012, http://www.PsychologyToday.com/blog/snow-white-doesnt-live-here-anymore/201201/the-secret-behind-womens-laughter

[9] "Why Playing With Your Kids is So Important." *Parenthood.com,* Accessed April 3, 2013, http://www.parenthood.com/article-topics/why_playing_with_your_kids_is_so_important.html/page/1

[10] Neh. 8:10